Annabel Karmel
Top 100 Finger Foods

Annabel Karmel
Top 100 Finger Foods

100 quick and easy meals for a healthy, happy child

EBURY PRESS

For my children Nicholas, Lara and Scarlett, and
Oscar, my puppy, who gets to enjoy the leftovers

10 9

Published in 2009 by Ebury Press, an imprint of Ebury Publishing

A Random House Group Company

Text copyright © Annabel Karmel 2009
Photography copyright © Dave King 2009

Annabel Karmel has asserted her right to be identified as the
author of this Work in accordance with the Copyright, Designs
and Patents Act 1988

All rights reserved. No part of this publication may be reproduced,
stored in a retrieval system, or transmitted in any form or by
any means, electronic, mechanical, photocopying, recording or
otherwise, without the prior permission of the copyright owner

The Random House Group Limited Reg. No. 954009

Addresses for companies within the Random House Group
can be found at **www.randomhouse.co.uk**

A CIP catalogue record for this book is available from the
British Library

The Random House Group Limited supports the Forest Stewardship
Council® (FSC®), the leading international forest-certification
organisation. Our books carrying the FSC label are printed on FSC®
-certified paper. FSC is the only forest-certification scheme supported by
the leading environmental organisations, including Greenpeace. Our paper
procurement policy can be found at www.randomhouse.co.uk/environment

To buy books by your favourite authors and register for offers visit
www.randomhouse.co.uk

Printed and bound in China by C&C Offset Printing Co.,Ltd

Colour origination by Altaimage, London

Design & illustrations: Smith & Gilmour, London
Photography: Dave King
Food stylist: Seiko Hatfield
Props stylist: Jo Harris
Copy editor: Helen Armitage

ISBN 978 0 09 192507 9

MIX
Paper from
responsible sources
FSC® C008047
FSC
www.fsc.org

Please note all flour is plain unless otherwise specifi… all butter is unsalted, milk is full fat and eggs are me…

Contents

Introduction

First Finger Foods

Until now, feeding your baby has been your job, but at around 8 or 9 months old your little one will start to want to do this on his own. Quite often babies are determined to feed themselves before they have the level of co-ordination required to use a spoon. This is an age when children experiment with their food, and if you are the type of person who likes everything neat and tidy you are going to have to draw a deep breath as your child will want to play with their food. They are going to want to touch, hold, drop and, occasionally, throw their food.

Finger foods are about to become an increasingly important part of your baby's diet, and the more you allow your child to experiment, the quicker they will learn to feed themselves. Don't be concerned if your child ends up wearing most of the food to begin with. At this early stage, it's simply practice. But do keep offering finger foods and more lumpy textures as this will help refine your baby's chewing technique, which in turn helps with speech development and strengthens your baby's jaw muscles. Interestingly, many babies refuse to eat lumpy food from a spoon or fork but will eat finger foods even though these also require chewing.

Good first finger foods

Initially it's important to choose foods that are quite soft as babies can bite off a piece of a hard food like raw carrot and choke on it – so, to start off, I like to offer the following:

- Steamed vegetables, such as carrot or sweet-potato sticks, small broccoli or cauliflower florets
- Soft ripe fruit: for example, banana, peach, melon, mango
- Toast soldiers or fingers of grilled cheese on toast
- Cooked pasta shapes with a very small amount of sauce or a little melted butter and grated cheese

Finger foods for older babies

Among the suggestions that follow, there are lots of accompanying recipes throughout the book from which to choose.

- Sticks of cheese
- Raw vegetables, for example carrot, cucumber sticks
- Apple slices, strawberries, blueberries halved peeled grapes
- Dried fruits, for example apricots, apples, raisins – use the soft ready-to-eat variety
- Unsweetened breakfast cereals
- Rice cakes
- Mini meatballs or burgers
- Pieces of chicken or fish with or without breadcrumbs
- Wafer-thin cooked meats, rolled up into a cigar shape

- Pitta bread, naan bread, bagel
- Mini sandwiches – mashed banana, cream cheese, peanut butter (provided there is no history of allergy in your family or atopic disease, for example hayfever, asthma or eczema, it should be fine to give peanut butter from 7 months old)
- Mini home-made pizzas
- Mini muffins
- Mini home-made cookies
- Mini ice lollies made from fresh fruit

Checklist for first finger foods

1 Peel apples and pears initially, but as your baby gets older, introduce the skin as well as the vitamins lie just below it.

2 Often it's better to give a large piece of fruit or vegetable that your child can hold and eat rather than bite-sized pieces.

3 When making sandwiches for little ones, it's a good idea to slightly flatten the bread first with a rolling pin so that the sandwich is not too thick for your child to eat.

4 There is no need to be obsessive about germs. It's fine to use an antibacterial wipe to clean your baby's high chair – but remember your baby picks things up from the floor and puts them in his mouth all the time.

5 Your baby's hands should always be washed before they eat.

6 One very common thing that paediatric dieticians talk about is children who are afraid of mess. This seems to be at the root of many toddler eating problems. Allow your baby to experiment – they are bound to get into a mess but it's not a good idea continually to wipe your child's face clean when they are eating.

7 Try not to buy dried apricots that are treated with sulphur dioxide to preserve their bright orange colour as this can trigger an asthma attack in susceptible babies.

8 A large mess mat placed under the high chair to catch food and recycle it is a good investment.

Choking

Just because your child can chew off a piece of food, like a chunk of raw carrot or apple, doesn't mean that they can chew it down properly. Sometimes children bite off pieces of food and then store them in their mouth, so always check when your child comes out of the high chair that there is no lumpy food left in their mouth.

Foods that are choking hazards include:
- pieces of raw vegetables
- grapes – you should peel grapes and cut them in half or into quarters
- raisins – these can get caught in the throat
- fruit with stones
- cherry tomatoes – best to quarter these
- chunks of hard cheese
- nuts

What to do if your child chokes:
- If your child chokes, check inside their mouth and remove any object, but be careful not to push the object further down the throat.
- Lay your baby face down on your forearm with their head lower than their chest. Give them five sharp slaps on the middle of their back with your other hand.
- If this does not dislodge the object, turn your baby over on to their back and, pushing down with two fingers in the middle of their chest, make five sharp thrusts at a rate of about one every 3 seconds. Then check your baby's mouth again for any obstruction.
- If unsuccessful, call the emergency services immediately.

Teething

Some babies are born with teeth, some get them at 6 months old, and some may have hardly any teeth by the time they are 1 year old. While some babies sail through teething, it can be a pretty miserable time for others. Telltale teething signs include bright red cheeks, inflamed gums, mild rash around the mouth, mild fever, irritability, changes in feeding and sleeping patterns. As a parent I believe it's very important to trust your instincts, and you know better than anyone when something is not right with your baby. There is divided opinion among experts on whether teething can cause a mild fever or diarrhoea. However, they all agree that you should check with your doctor or health visitor if you are concerned about your baby and don't just put it down to teething.

Some ways to help your baby:

While your baby is teething it is not unusual for them to be off their food. It is a good idea to keep some chilled cucumber sticks in the fridge, put banana in the freezer or make some fresh fruit ice lollies. Cold foods help to soothe sore gums. You can also dampen some clean washcloths, freeze them and then offer them to your child to chew on.

Offer your child some cool, smooth foods like apple purée, yoghurt or fromage frais.

Gel-filled teething rings that can be put in the fridge can also help cool sore gums.

You can rub sugar-free teething gel on your baby's gums or give some sugar-free paracetamol if your baby has a slight fever.

Homeopathic granules that babies crunch against their gums can be a relief for teething babies.

Cuddle or nurse your baby – a baby feels less uncomfortable if relaxed and happy. Try to distract them by offering a change in scenery, a new toy or a fun activity – it will make it harder for them to concentrate on being miserable.

Rub Vaseline or petroleum jelly around the outside of your baby's mouth to protect it from becoming red and sore when your baby dribbles.

Make sure that you brush your child's teeth as soon as they appear. Use a baby toothbrush and a smear of fluoride toothpaste.

Try to avoid sugary drinks. Only give milk or water in a bottle. However, you can give juice at mealtimes in a beaker but make sure it has no added sugar. It is best to restrict juice to mealtimes when there is plenty of saliva in the mouth to wash away the acid.

Breakfast Bites

A good breakfast should contain protein such as eggs, cheese or yoghurt, wholegrain cereal or bread and some fresh fruit. Your idea of breakfast is bound to be different from your child's. Be flexible – my children have been known to eat odd things for breakfast like split, toasted muffins spread with tomato sauce and topped with tomatoes and grated Cheddar then popped under the grill. If there's a rush in the morning and no time to sit and eat breakfast, give your child a healthy fruit muffin and a smoothie to take with them on their journey.

Fluffy Finger-sized Pancakes

🍲 Preparation 7 minutes
🕐 Cook 20 minutes (assuming 5 batches)
🍳 Makes approx. 24 small/8 large pancakes or 4–6 portions
☺ Suitable for children under 1 year old

50 g (2 oz) self-raising flour
1 tbsp caster sugar
¼ tsp bicarbonate of soda
a pinch of salt (optional)
1 egg
3 tbsp milk
1 tbsp oil, for frying
4 tbsp natural or vanilla yoghurt
2 tsp maple syrup

American-style pancakes are yummy for breakfast and also make a nice dessert for both kids and adults. Try them with fruits, such as sliced bananas, strawberries or blueberries, too.

Stir the flour, sugar, bicarbonate of soda and salt (if using) together in a medium bowl. Beat the egg and milk together in a separate bowl and add to the dry ingredients then mix together until just combined. Leave the batter to stand for 5 minutes – it will thicken slightly, and you will see some bubbles forming.

Meanwhile heat a large, heavy-based frying pan over a medium heat. Brush a little oil on the base and drop teaspoonfuls of the batter into the pan. For larger pancakes, use tablespoonfuls of batter. Cook for 1½–2 minutes, until the pancakes are golden on the base and bubbles have formed on the surface. Flip over and cook for a further 1–2 minutes, until the pancakes are cooked through and brown on the second side. Lower the heat slightly if they are browning too quickly.

Transfer the cooked pancakes to a plate and keep warm in a low oven. Re-oil the pan and continue cooking batches of the pancakes, until all of the batter has been used up.

Divide the yoghurt among four small bowls and drizzle half a teaspoon of maple syrup over the top of each. Serve with the warm pancakes.

Suitable for freezing: cool the cooked pancakes and wrap in foil packets. Reheat direct from frozen in an oven pre-heated to 200°C/400°F/Gas 6/Fan 180°C. Put the foil packet(s) on a baking sheet and bake for 5–6 minutes. Cool slightly before serving.

Breakfast Burrito

A burrito generally describes a filling completely enclosed by a flour tortilla or wrap. It gets its name from Mexico, where it was a popular 'packed lunch' for travelling (*burro* is Spanish for donkey). But nowadays they are popular all over America, especially for breakfast. For a mild salsa recipe, see Nachos (p. 27), or use your favourite shop-bought one.

Whisk the egg and milk/cream together in a small bowl and season to taste with salt and pepper. Melt the butter in a small pan and add the egg mixture. Cook gently, stirring, until the eggs are softly scrambled.

Warm the tortilla for 10–15 seconds in a microwave or for 1 minute in a dry frying pan. Spoon the scrambled egg down the centre of the tortilla (not quite to the edges of the wrap at the top and bottom) and then add the salsa and cheese. Fold the top and bottom of the wrap inwards then roll the wrap up from the left-hand side, so that the filling is completely enclosed. Serve immediately.

Preparation 5 minutes
Cook 5 minutes
Makes 1 portion
Not suitable for freezing or reheating

1 egg
1 tbsp milk or cream
a knob of butter
1 flour tortilla wrap
1 tbsp mild salsa or ½ tomato, seeded and diced
15 g (½ oz) Cheddar, grated
salt and pepper, to season

Optional add-ins
You can ring the changes by adding extra fillings to the basic recipe above. Some of my favourites are:

1 rasher bacon, cooked until crisp and crumbled
1 cooked new potato, diced and sautéed in a little oil until golden
1 small slice ham, cut into cubes or small strips
1 tbsp drained canned sweetcorn, added to the eggs so that it heats through
2–3 mushrooms, thinly sliced and sautéed in a little oil

Soft-boiled Eggs with 'Italian Soldiers'

Preparation 5 minutes
Cook 4 minutes
Makes 1 portion (easily increased)

1 egg
2 breadsticks
2 slices prosciutto or Parma ham

My new twist on a nursery favourite of eggs and soldiers. I like to vary this by sometimes using sesame-coated breadsticks. The 'Italian Soldiers' would also make a nice change for a lunchbox, in double quantity. Do not, though, give lightly cooked eggs to babies under the age of one.

Put a large pan of water on a high heat and bring to the boil then reduce the heat slightly to a brisk simmer. Gently lower in the egg, using a spoon, and cook the egg for 4 minutes (for a runny yolk and a set white).

Meanwhile, break the breadsticks in half and cut the slices of prosciutto in half lengthways. Wrap one of the pieces of prosciutto around one of the breadstick halves, starting at the broken or cut end, and wrap twisting downwards and slightly overlapping, so that around two-thirds of the breadstick is wrapped in ham. Press the ham firmly on itself to seal. Repeat so that you have four 'Italian Soldiers'.

Transfer the egg to an egg cup and cut off the top. Dip the 'Italian Soldiers' in the egg yolk and enjoy!

Welsh 'Rabbits'

Welsh rarebit is a slightly enriched version of cheese on toast – children will probably enjoy this version of 'rabbit'.

Pre-heat the grill to High. Put the cheese, egg, cream/milk and Worcestershire sauce into a bowl and mash together. Season to taste with pepper. Spread the cheese mixture over the cut sides of the toasted muffins, spreading right to the edges. Grill for 3–4 minutes, until the cheese has melted and is golden and bubbling. Split the muffin and cook the two pieces under the grill around 7–8 cm (about 3 in) away from the heat source (one rack down from normal grilling position) – don't have them too close as the egg in the mixture can make them brown very quickly.

Decorate the cooked muffins with peas for eyes and strips of carrot, mangetout or snow peas for ears, half an olive for a nose and chives for whiskers. Serve immediately.

🍲 Preparation 5 minutes
🕐 Cook 7 minutes
🍥 Makes 1 portion
❄ Not suitable for freezing or reheating

1 muffin
45 g (1½ oz) Cheddar, grated
1 egg yolk
1 tsp cream or milk
2–3 drops Worcestershire sauce (or to taste)
pepper, to season
thin slices of carrot, 1 black olive (stoned and halved), peas, mangetout (optional) and a few fresh chives, to garnish

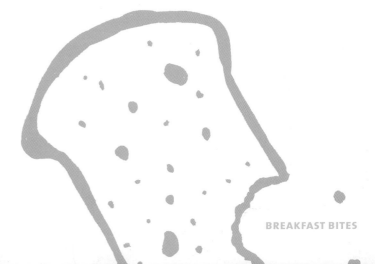

French Toast Fingers

🍽 Preparation 7 minutes
🕐 Cook 6 minutes
🍽 Makes 1–2 portions,
depending on age and appetite
☺ Suitable for children under
1 year old
❄ Not suitable for freezing
or reheating

2 slices white bread
1 tbsp strawberry or
    raspberry jam
1 tbsp reduced-fat soft
    cheese (optional)
1 egg
1 tbsp cream or milk
½ tsp caster sugar
2 drops vanilla extract
10 g (½ oz) butter, for frying

I like to use white bread, but feel free to use wholemeal.
You can buy some very good sugar-free jam.

Roll the bread with a rolling pin until about half its original
thickness and spread one slice with the jam. Spread the second
slice with cream cheese (if using) and sandwich together. Trim
off the crusts, if liked. Beat the egg, cream/milk, sugar and
vanilla together in a shallow dish.

Melt the butter in a frying pan over a medium heat. Dip the
jam sandwich into the egg mixture and turn over to coat. Put
the egg-coated sandwich into the pan and fry for 2–3 minutes,
until the underside is golden. Flip over and cook for a further
2–3 minutes then transfer to a plate and carefully cut into
fingers (a small serrated knife is good for this).

Allow to cool slightly and check the temperature before
serving – be careful as the jam can become very hot.

Mini Banana Bran Muffins

🍽 Preparation 10 minutes
🕐 Cook 12 minutes
🍽 Makes 24 muffins
☺ Suitable for children under
1 year old
❄ Not suitable for reheating

50 g (2 oz) Bran Flakes
75 ml (3½ fl oz) warm milk
1 medium banana, mashed

There always seems to be the odd brown banana lurking in the
bottom of the fruit bowl, and this is a great way to use it up.
These are wonderful warm for breakfast or for a teatime snack.

Pre-heat the oven to 180°C/350°F/Gas 4/Fan 160°C.

Line two 12-hole mini-muffin tins with 24 paper cases.
Mix together the Bran Flakes, milk and banana, and leave
for 5 minutes. Transfer to a food processor with the egg
yolk, oil, raisins and sugar. Whiz for a minute to combine.

Add the flour, bicarbonate of soda, baking powder, salt, cinnamon and ginger, and pulse to combine. Spoon into the mini-muffin cases (about one tablespoon for each mini muffin). Bake for 12–14 minutes until risen and firm to the touch. Remove from the oven and allow to cool for 5 minutes, then transfer to a wire rack to cool completely.

Suitable for freezing: baked muffins are best stored frozen. Freeze in a re-sealable box or freezer bag. Defrost for around 30 minutes at room temperature.

1 egg yolk
50 ml (2 fl oz) sunflower oil
50 g (2 oz) raisins
60 g (2½ oz) soft light brown
   sugar
60 g (2½ oz) wholemeal
   plain flour
½ tsp bicarbonate of soda
½ tsp baking powder
a generous pinch of salt
½ tsp ground cinnamon
¼ tsp ground ginger

Eggy Bread with Caramelised Bananas

Mix together the cream, milk, eggs and vanilla. Cut the bread into triangles or fingers and put in a small, flat dish. Pour the egg mixture on top and leave to soak for 5 minutes, turning over halfway.

Heat a knob of butter in a frying pan and allow to melt. Put the bread in the pan and fry gently over a low heat for about 5 minutes on each side or until lightly golden.

Fry the bananas. Melt the butter in a small frying pan. Add the sugar. Add the bananas and fry gently until caramelised. Cool the bananas slightly before serving as caramelised sugar can get very hot. Serve the eggy bread with the bananas and sprinkle with a little caster sugar.

Preparation 12 minutes
Cook 10 minutes
Makes 2 portions
Suitable for children under 1
Not suitable for freezing or reheating

50 ml (2 fl oz) double cream
50 ml (2 fl oz) milk
2 eggs
2–3 drops vanilla extract
1 thick slice white bread, preferably
   from an unsliced loaf
a knob of butter, for frying
caster sugar, to sprinkle

For the caramelised bananas
10 g (½ oz) butter
10 g (½ oz) caster sugar
2 bananas, peeled and cut into
   thick slices on the angle

Versatile Veg

Children need proportionately more fat than adults so for them a vegetarian diet should include foods such as cheese and eggs as well as avocados, nut butters and seeds. Lack of iron is the most common deficiency in vegetarian children, so be sure to give iron-rich green leafy vegetables, egg yolk, fortified breakfast cereals and dried fruit, especially apricots. Vitamin C-rich foods or a glass of orange juice with a meal helps boost iron absorption.

Carrot and Cheese Muffins

🍲 Preparation 15 minutes
🕐 Cook 16 minutes
🧁 Makes 18 mini or 6 large muffins
❄ Muffins can be fozen in a re-sealable box or freezer bag. Defrost for 30–45 minutes at room temperature. Not suitable for reheating

85 g (3 oz) self-raising flour
¼ tsp bicarbonate of soda
a pinch of salt
a pinch of paprika
30 g (1 oz) Cheddar, grated
30 g (1 oz) Parmesan, freshly grated, plus 2 tbsp extra for topping
2 tbsp milk
2 tbsp sunflower oil
4 tbsp natural yoghurt
1 tbsp maple syrup
1 egg
1 medium carrot, peeled and finely grated
1 tsp snipped chives (optional)

Carrot is good in sweet muffins but equally nice in savoury ones too. It is a good way to hide a few extra vegetables to help you get your child to eat their healthy 5-a-day.

Pre-heat the oven to 180°C/350°F/Gas 4/Fan 160°C. Line mini-muffin tins with 18 paper cases.

Stir the flour, bicarbonate of soda, salt, paprika and cheeses together in a bowl. Beat the milk, oil, yoghurt, maple syrup and egg together, and stir into the dry ingredients, followed by the carrot and chives. Drop heaped teaspoonfuls into the prepared muffin tins (fill paper cases almost to the top). Sprinkle over the remaining Parmesan and bake for 14–16 minutes for mini muffins, 25–30 minutes for large, until risen and golden brown.

Remove from the oven and allow to cool for 5 minutes, then transfer to a wire rack to cool completely.

Cheese and Sweetcorn Muffins

Savoury muffins are a slight change but all the better for it.
I like to serve these as a mid-morning snack or breakfast,
or, for older children, with soup for lunch.

Pre-heat the oven to 180°C/350°F/Gas 4/Fan 160°C. Line two
12-hole mini-muffin tins with 24 paper cases. Put the sweetcorn
and spring onions in a food processor and whiz until chopped.
Add the yoghurt, butter, honey and egg, and whiz to combine.
Sift together the flour, bicarbonate of soda, baking powder, salt
and paprika, add to the yoghurt mixture together with the
grated cheese and pulse two or three times.

Spoon into the mini-muffin cases (about three-quarters
of a tablespoon per case). Bake for 12–14 minutes or until risen
and firm to the touch. Allow to cool in the tin for a few minutes
then transfer to a wire rack to cool completely.

Preparation 10 minutes
Cook 14 minutes
Makes 24 muffins
Suitable for freezing:
baked muffins can be fozen
in a re-sealable box or freezer
bag. Defrost for 30–45 minutes
at room temperature. Not
suitable for reheating

85 g (3 oz) drained canned
    sweetcorn
3 spring onions, roughly sliced
4 tbsp Greek yoghurt
30 g (1 oz) butter, melted and
    cooled
1 tbsp clear honey or maple syrup
1 egg
85 g (3 oz) flour (or 50 g/2 oz
    flour and 35 g/1 oz cornmeal)
1/2 tsp bicarbonate of soda
1/2 tsp baking powder
1/4 tsp salt
1/8 tsp paprika
50 g (2 oz) mature Cheddar,
    grated

Veggie Bites/Burgers

🍳 Preparation 20 minutes
🕐 Cook 12 minutes
🍩 Makes about 16 small bites
or 8 burgers
☺ Suitable for children under 1
❄ Suitable for freezing: freeze
uncooked bites/burgers on baking
sheets lined with non-stick baking
parchment. When firm transfer
to re-sealable freezer bags. Cook
direct from frozen, adding 1 minute's
extra cooking time for bites and
2 minutes' extra for burgers.

2 tbsp olive oil
1 medium shallot, diced
½ stick celery, diced
1 large carrot, peeled and grated
½ small leek, finely sliced
3 chestnut mushrooms, diced
1 garlic clove, crushed
1 tbsp dark soy sauce
2 tsp soft light brown sugar
4 tbsp freshly grated Parmesan
40 g (1½ oz) fresh breadcrumbs
½ tbsp mayonnaise
15 g (½ oz) Cheddar, grated
5 tbsp dried breadcrumbs
2 tbsp flour
1 egg
2–3 tbsp sunflower oil, for frying
salt and pepper, to season
buns, lettuce, tomato, mayonnaise,
    to serve (for burgers)

Ever met a vegetable-hating vegetarian? Well, I have met quite a few. These tasty veggie bites or burgers are a good way to encourage children to eat more vegetables as here they are mashed up – and not being visible they can't be picked out.

Heat the olive oil in a large non-stick pan and sauté the vegetables for 10 minutes, until soft. Add the garlic and cook for a minute, then add the soy sauce and sugar, and cook for a further minute. Spread out on a plate and leave to cool.

For the small veggie bites/burgers you need to chop the cooked and cooled veg, either in a food processor (scraping down the sides frequently), or with a large knife.

Transfer the vegetables to a bowl and mix in two tablespoons of the Parmesan, the fresh breadcrumbs, mayonnaise and Cheddar and pepper to taste (the soy sauce should give enough salt). For the bites take teaspoonfuls and roll into balls. For burgers take tablespoonfuls and squish into a patty shape. If you have time, put on a plate and chill for 1 hour or, preferably, overnight. However, they can be coated and cooked without chilling.

Mix together the dried breadcrumbs and rest of the Parmesan on a large plate, along with salt and pepper to taste. Put the plain flour on a plate and season with salt and pepper. Beat the egg in a small bowl.

Dust the bites/burgers in the seasoned flour then dip in egg and roll in the breadcrumbs. Heat the sunflower oil in a large non-stick pan and cook the bites/burgers for 1–2 minutes each side, until golden. Drain on kitchen paper and serve warm – with buns, lettuce, tomato and mayonnaise for burgers.

Nachos

I find that I have to make little individual nachos as my children always end up arguing over who is eating the most, and this is the only way I can guarantee they all get the same! However, you can just pile the tortilla chips together in the centre of the foil and scatter over the salsa and cheese, then grill and just let everyone help themselves. It is also really easy to make double quantities (or more) if you need to please a crowd. I like to make my own fresh salsa but you can always use four tablespoons of your favourite shop-bought one instead.

To make the salsa, mix all of the ingredients together in a small bowl and season to taste with salt and pepper. Cover and chill until needed – it will keep for up to 2 days in the fridge.

To make the nachos, pre-heat the grill to High and line a grill pan with foil. Sit the tortilla chips on the foil and top each one with half a teaspoon of salsa and a little of the cheese. Grill for 1–2 minutes, until the cheese has just melted. Watch carefully as the edges of the tortilla chips can burn easily.

Transfer the nachos to two plates and top each one with a small blob of soured cream, if using. Serve immediately, with the salsa.

Preparation 10 minutes
Cook 2 minutes
Makes 2 portions
Not suitable for freezing or reheating

For the mild salsa
1 large tomato, skinned, seeded and diced
1 spring onion, thinly sliced
2 tsp chopped fresh coriander (or to taste)
1 tsp fresh lime juice
salt and pepper, to season

For the nachos
12 (30 g/1 oz) plain tortilla chips
30 g (1 oz) Cheddar, grated
1 tbsp soured cream (optional)

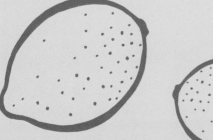

Tortilla Pizza Margherita

📛 Preparation 5 minutes
🕐 Cook 9 minutes
🌀 Makes 1 portion
❄ Not suitable for freezing
or reheating

1 wheat tortilla wrap
2½ tbsp tomato sauce
30 g (1 oz) Cheddar or
    mozzarella, grated

**Toppings Menu (I would suggest
no more than 2 toppings per
pizza, if using)**
2–3 black stoned olives, cut
    into rings
1 cherry tomato, cut into rings
2 cubes drained canned
    pineapple, cut into dice
1 tbsp diced red pepper
1 tbsp drained canned sweetcorn
1 spring onion, sliced
2 mushrooms, sliced and
    sautéed in a little oil
3–4 very thin slices courgette,
    brushed with a little oil before
    putting on pizza
1 tbsp freshly grated Parmesan
2 SunBlush tomatoes, cut into
    small pieces

I love thin-crust pizzas, and wheat tortilla wraps make an ideal 'instant' base – turning deliciously crisp in the oven. They are also perfect for smaller children who find the slimmer base easier to eat. Sometimes the air bubbles in the wrap puff up a bit as the pizza bakes – but they deflate as soon as they come out of the oven, so don't panic! You can use your favourite tomato-sauce recipe or shop-bought sauce, or try my recipe for a Quick Tomato Sauce (see p. 32).

Pre-heat the oven to 200°C/400°F/Gas 6/Fan 180°C.

Put the tortilla wrap on a baking sheet and spread over the tomato sauce. Sprinkle over the cheese. You can also add any toppings that your child may like (see suggestions left). Bake for 8–9 minutes, until the cheese has melted and the base is crisp. Cut into triangles and allow to cool slightly before serving.

Arancini with Quick Tomato Sauce

Arancini are a popular snack in Italy and were originally invented by thrifty Italians to use up leftover risotto. I have just used the ordinary grated mozzarella here as it is a bit drier than normal mozzarella and helps to make the base mixture stickier.

Melt the butter in a large pan and sauté the shallot for 2–3 minutes, until translucent. Add the garlic and rice, and cook, stirring constantly, for a further 2 minutes. Add 400 ml (14 fl oz) of the stock and bring to the boil, then reduce the heat to a simmer. Cook the rice for 20–25 minutes until just tender. Stir every 4–5 minutes and add a little extra stock if it becomes too dry.

Remove the pan from the heat and stir in the cheeses. Season to taste with a little pepper (you are unlikely to need extra salt). Spread the risotto out on a large plate and leave to cool, then cover and chill as quickly as possible.

Take slightly rounded teaspoonfuls of cold risotto and roll into balls. Season the breadcrumbs with salt and pepper and a little paprika (if using). Put the flour on a plate and the egg in a small bowl. Dust the risotto balls with flour, dip in egg and coat in breadcrumbs then place on a baking sheet lined with cling film.

Put enough oil into a large frying pan to give a depth of 1 cm (½ in) and put over a medium heat. When the oil is shimmering add the arancini and fry for 6–8 minutes, turning frequently, until golden brown. Drain on a plate lined with kitchen paper. Serve with tomato sauce (see pp. 32 and 33) for dipping.

Preparation 15 minutes, plus cooling and chilling
Cook 25 minutes for rice, plus 16 minutes frying
Makes approx. 28 arancini or 7–9 portions (recipe easily halved)
Suitable for freezing: cover the baking sheet with cling film and freeze the arancini until firm then transfer to a re-sealable bag. Cook direct from frozen, on a medium–low heat increasing the cooking time to 10–12 minutes. Check that the centres are piping hot then allow to cool slightly before serving.

10 g (½ oz) butter
1 small shallot, finely chopped
½ small garlic clove, crushed
110 g (4 oz) risotto rice
500 ml (17 fl oz) hot vegetable or chicken stock
30 g (1 oz) grated mozzarella
30 g (1 oz) mature Cheddar, grated
3 tbsp freshly grated Parmesan
50 g (2 oz) dried breadcrumbs
a pinch of paprika (optional)
2 tbsp flour
1 egg, beaten
sunflower oil, for frying
salt and pepper, to season

Quick Tomato Sauce

🍲 Preparation 5 minutes
🕐 Cook 22 minutes
🥧 Makes 3–4 portions

1 tbsp olive oil
1 shallot, diced
1 garlic clove, crushed
1 x 400 g can chopped tomatoes
1 tsp brown sugar
1 tbsp tomato ketchup
salt and pepper, to season

Use half to accompany the arancini (see p. 31) – the rest freezes well and can be served with pasta or used as a topping for pizza.

Heat the oil in a large frying pan, and sauté the shallot and garlic for 2 minutes, stirring constantly. Add the remaining ingredients and bring to a boil, squashing the tomatoes with the back of a wooden spoon. Boil for 15 minutes, stirring frequently, until the sauce has thickened. Season to taste with salt and pepper.

Garlic and Herb Dip

🍲 Preparation 5 minutes
🥧 Makes 3–4 portions
❄ Not suitable for freezing
or reheating

3 tbsp mayonnaise
1 tbsp Greek yoghurt
1 tsp milk
¼ tsp crushed garlic
¼ tsp fresh lemon juice
1 tsp finely chopped fresh
   parsley (or you could use
   fresh coriander or dill)

Children tend to like garlic more than we might expect, and this dip is delicious with lots of things – breadsticks, carrot and cucumber sticks, Buffalo Wings (see p. 95), fish or chicken goujons (see pp. 58 and 77), pitta-bread fingers.

Simply mix all the ingredients together with a pinch of salt. The dip will keep stored in the fridge for up to 3 days.

Cherry Tomato Sauce

This would make a good dipping sauce for other vegetarian dishes, such as Mini Vegetable Balls (p. 53), Grilled Vegetable Skewers (p. 36), Arancini (p. 31), Veggie Bites/Burgers (p. 24), Baked Mozzarella Sticks (p. 45), or, for non-vegetarians, for the Krispie Chicken Nuggets (p. 77) or Annabel's Chicken Rissoles (p. 80).

Pre-heat the oven to 180°C/350°F/160°C Fan/Gas 4.

Halve the cherry tomatoes and put in a small roasting tin. Sprinkle over the thyme leaves and drizzle over one tablespoon of the olive oil. Tuck the garlic in the centre and roast for 20 minutes.

Meanwhile, sauté the shallot in the remaining oil for 5 minutes. Add the tomatoes, both tomato purées and sugar, and simmer for 10 minutes. Add the roasted cherry tomatoes and cook for a further 30 minutes. Blitz in a food processor or blender. If you want a very smooth sauce you could then press this through a sieve.

Preparation 10 minutes
Cook 50 minutes
Makes 4 portions
Suitable for freezing and reheating. Cool and freeze in re-sealable container. Defrost at room temperature for 2–3 hours or in a microwave for 2–3 minutes. Can be reheated in a pan over a gentle heat for 5 minutes or for approximately 2 minutes in a microwave, until piping hot.

300 g (11 oz) plum cherry
   tomatoes
1/4 tsp fresh thyme leaves
2 tbsp olive oil
1 garlic clove, halved
1 large shallot, diced
1 x 400 g can chopped tomatoes
2 tbsp tomato purée
1 tbsp sun-dried tomato purée
1 tsp sugar

Potato Pizzette Bites

🖐 Preparation 5 minutes
🕐 Cook 25 minutes
🍲 Makes 2 portions (easily doubled)
❄ Not suitable for freezing or reheating

1 large waxy-type potato, skin on and thoroughly washed (Desirée, or similar)
1 tbsp olive oil
3 tbsp tomato sauce (try Quick Tomato Sauce, p. 32)
50 g (2 oz) Cheddar or mozzarella, grated
salt and pepper, to season

Slices of crisp potato make an unusual base for small finger-sized pizzas or pizzette

Pre-heat the oven to 200°C/400°F/Gas 6/Fan 180°C.

Cut eight large slices of potato, cutting crosswise from the centre of the potato, each around 2 mm/1/12 in thick. You won't need the thinner end bits of the potato, but these will keep for up to 2 days in the fridge, covered with cold water, and can be used for mashed or boiled potatoes.

Brush each potato slice with oil and season with a little salt and pepper. Lay the slices on a baking sheet lined with non-stick baking parchment and bake for 10 minutes. Turn the slices over and bake for a further 8–10 minutes, until golden and crisp. Watch carefully for the last 2–3 minutes.

Top each potato slice with around one teaspoon of tomato sauce and scatter over the cheese. Bake for a further 5–7 minutes, or grill for 2–3 minutes, until the cheese has melted. Cool slightly before serving.

Grilled Vegetable Skewers

🍲 Preparation 8 minutes
🕐 Cook 10 minutes
🎂 Makes 4 skewers or 2–4 portions
☺ Suitable for children under 1 year old
❄ Not suitable for freezing or reheating but can be eaten cold.

¼ large red pepper
¼ large orange pepper
½ medium green courgette
½ medium yellow courgette
   (or green if unavailable)

For the marinade
2 tbsp olive oil
2 tsp balsamic vinegar
1 tsp sugar
salt and pepper, to season
You will also need 4 wooden
   skewers, soaked in warm
   water for 20 minutes

Marinating the vegetables in a balsamic vinaigrette helps to accentuate their natural sweetness and can make them more appealing to kids. The vegetables are delicious warm and leftovers are yummy added to tomato pasta sauces or to salads (see my Mix 'n' Match Pasta Salad, p. 117).

Cut off the tops of the peppers and remove the core and seeds. Cut into slices to make rings. Slice four circles from each courgette (approximately 1 cm/¼ in thick) and cut each circle across in half to give eight semicircles each of green and yellow courgette.

Put the marinade ingredients into a medium bowl and whisk together. Season to taste with salt and pepper then add the vegetables and toss to coat. Marinate for a minimum of 2 hours or overnight, stirring the vegetables occasionally.

Pre-heat the grill to High and line a grill pan with foil. Thread pieces of pepper and courgette on to the skewers. Put the skewers on the foil and brush over some of the remaining marinade. Grill for 4–5 minutes, until the vegetables start to soften around the edges – watch carefully as they can brown very quickly if they are too close to the heat source.

Turn the skewers over and brush with more marinade. Grill for a further 4–5 minutes, until the vegetables are cooked through. Again watch carefully and lower the grill rack if the vegetables are browning too quickly. The skewers can also be barbecued over medium hot coals.

Allow the skewers to cool slightly before serving. Leftover vegetables can be removed from the skewers and stored, covered, in the fridge for up to 2 days.

Petit Panini

Preparation 5 minutes
Cook 7 minutes
Makes 1 portion (for an older child)
Not suitable for freezing or reheating

10 g (½ oz) butter, softened
1 hot-dog roll, split
2 slices tomato
2 slices mozzarella
1 tsp olive oil
salt and pepper, to season

Panini are delicious Italian toasted sandwiches, usually made with small loaves of bread. I like to use hot-dog rolls, as they are a perfect size for children.

Spread the butter on the cut sides of the roll. Lay the tomato and mozzarella on the bottom of the roll, season, and make into a sandwich using the top of the roll. Pre-heat a griddle pan and grease with the olive oil. Put the panini top side down on the grill and press down well. Cook for 3–4 minutes until golden and crisp. Turn over the panini and cook for a further 3 minutes until warmed through. Cut in half and serve.

Falafel with Minty Yoghurt Dressing

Preparation 20 minutes
Cook 8 minutes (assuming 2 batches)
Makes 4–6 portions
Not suitable for freezing but can be reheated in a microwave for approximately 1 minute – and also good cold.

1 small onion, finely chopped
1 tbsp olive oil
1 small garlic clove, crushed
¼–½ tsp ground cumin

As with meat-eaters, the key to a healthy vegetarian diet is to eat a wide range of foods. This is particularly true for vegetarians because, apart from a few foods like quinoa and tofu, most plant proteins are not complete and only by eating a variety of them can you optimise your protein intake. Falafel are equally delicious cold so they are a good lunchbox option. Chick-peas are also a good source of vegetable protein.

Sauté the onion in the olive oil for 8–10 minutes, until soft. Add the garlic, cumin and coriander, and cook for a further 2 minutes. While the onion is cooking drain the tinned chick-peas and rinse with cold water. Turn the chick-peas on to kitchen paper and rub dry then transfer to a bowl, leaving behind as many of the papery skins as possible.

Mash the chick-peas with a potato masher then stir in the onion, parsley, lemon zest and houmous, and season to taste with salt and pepper. Divide the mixture into 12 (scant tablespoons) and squash firmly into balls then press slightly to make small burger shapes. Dust with the flour and pat off any excess.

Heat the oil in a large frying pan and fry the falafel for 1–1½ minutes each side, until golden. Drain briefly on kitchen paper. Mix together the yoghurt, mint and lemon juice with a pinch of salt. (Dip and cooked falafel can be stored, covered, in the fridge for 2 days.)

Toast and split the pittas or warm the wraps. Spread over a tablespoon of the yoghurt dressing, and add two falafels and a little lettuce (if using). You can serve these with extra lemon wedges to squeeze over.

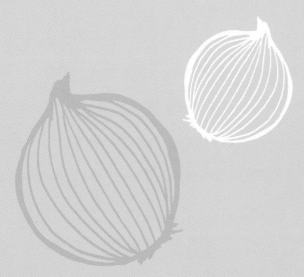

¼–½ tsp ground coriander
1 x 410 g can chick-peas
½ tbsp chopped parsley
finely grated zest 1 small lemon
3 tbsp houmous
1 tbsp flour
3 tbsp sunflower oil, for frying
salt and pepper, to season
4–6 pitta breads or wraps, shredded lettuce, lemon wedges, to serve (optional)

For the minty yoghurt dressing
6 tbsp Greek yoghurt
1 tsp (10–12 leaves) chopped fresh mint
1 tsp fresh lemon juice
a pinch of salt

TIP
You can ring the changes a bit by using different varieties of houmous (e.g. roasted pepper). I have suggested serving these in a wrap or pitta if warm, but you can also just serve them on their own, in which case you need to add a tablespoon of milk to the yoghurt to make it a little thinner.

Mushroom Pâté

🍳 Preparation 8 minutes,
plus cooling
🕐 Cook 12 minutes
🍥 Makes 4 portions
❄ Not suitable for freezing
or reheating

1 tbsp olive oil
200 g (7 oz) mushrooms,
   cleaned and thinly sliced
1 small garlic clove, crushed
¼ tsp fresh lemon juice
50 g (2 oz) soft cheese
salt and pepper, to season

Children who won't normally eat mushrooms may try this paté if they don't know what is in it! It is also a great option for vegetarians. I like it best spread thinly on to hot, fresh toast.

Heat the oil in a large frying pan and sauté the mushrooms for 8–10 minutes, until they are soft and any liquid released has evaporated. Add the garlic and cook for a further 2 minutes. Transfer the mushrooms to a food processor and allow to cool to room temperature.

Whiz the cooled mushrooms until finely chopped then add the remaining ingredients and whiz again to form a smooth pâté. Season to taste with salt and pepper then transfer to a container, cover and chill until needed. The pâté will keep for up to 3 days in the fridge.

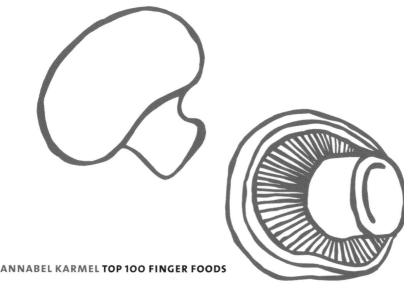

Oven-baked Potato Wedges

Oven-baked potato wedges are a healthy alternative to chips – I have left the skin on the potato as it contains a lot of extra vitamins and fibre. You can make spicy wedges by adding the optional paprika or fajita seasoning. These are particularly good served with my Garlic and Herb Dip (see p. 32).

Pre-heat the oven to 200°C/400°F/Gas 6/Fan 180°C.

Cut the potato lengthways into eight wedges. Put the oil in a bowl and season with a little salt and pepper plus the paprika, if using (for spicy wedges). Add the wedges and toss them in the oil.

Lay the wedges on a baking sheet lined with non-stick baking parchment and bake for 10 minutes, then turn them over and bake for a further 10 minutes. Turn over again and bake for a further 5–10 minutes, until the wedges are golden and cooked through.

Cool slightly before serving. Can be stored in the fridge, cooked, for 1 day. Reheat for 5 minutes in an oven pre-heated to 200°C/400°F/Gas 6/Fan 180°C.

🍽 Preparation 5 minutes
🕐 Cook 25 minutes
🍲 Makes 2 portions (easily doubled)
❄ Not suitable for freezing, but can be reheated in an oven pre-heated to 200°C/400°F/Gas 6/Fan 180°C for 5 minutes.

1 medium potato (e.g. Desirée or Yukon Gold), skin on and washed thoroughly
1/2 tbsp olive oil
1/4 tsp paprika or fajita seasoning (optional)
salt and pepper, to season

TIP
I line the baking sheet with non-stick baking parchment as otherwise the wedges tend to stick to the baking sheet. I have left the spicing as optional as not everyone will like it. You may prefer to prepare half the wedges spiced and half plain.

Cheese and Tomato Mini Quiches

🍲 Preparation 20 minutes
🕐 Cook 20 minutes
🍥 Makes 8 mini quiches
❄ Suitable for freezing: freeze cooked and chilled quiches in a re-sealable plastic box. Defrost overnight in the fridge. Reheat for 20–30 seconds in the microwave or for 8–10 minutes in an oven preheated to 150°C/300°F/Gas 2/Fan 130°C.

200 g (7 oz) ready rolled shortcrust pastry
8 cherry tomatoes (I used plum cherry tomatoes)
1 egg
6 tbsp milk
1 tbsp cream (or extra milk)
2 tbsp freshly grated Parmesan
45 g (1½ oz) mature Cheddar, grated
salt and pepper, to season

I like to use cherry tomatoes in these little quiches as they are deliciously sweet, and complement the cheesey filling well. For smaller children you can serve the quiches cut into quarters.

Use a 9 cm/3½ in round cutter to cut out eight pastry circles (re-roll trimmings if necessary). Press the pastry carefully into eight cups of a muffin tin and chill for 10 minutes. Alternatively you can make these in mini-quiche tins. Meanwhile pre-heat the oven to 200°C/400°F/Gas 6/Fan 180°C.

Cut each cherry tomato into quarters and set aside. Beat together the egg, milk, cream/extra milk and Parmesan, and season with a little salt (the Parmesan is quite salty) and pepper. Put four tomato quarters in the base of each pastry case. Spoon over the egg mixture (approximately one tablespoon per case) then top with the Cheddar.

Bake for 20 minutes, until the pastry is golden and the filling is set. Leave to cool in the tin for 10 minutes then run a knife around the edge of each tart and gently ease out of the tin. Serve warm or cold. Can be kept in the fridge for up to 2 days.

Sweetcorn Pancakes

🍲 Preparation 5 minutes
🕐 Cook 12 minutes (assuming 3 batches)
🍳 Makes 10–12 pancakes
❄ Suitable for freezing: put individual portions of 2–3 pancakes in a singe layer on pieces of foil and fold up to make a packet. Freeze. To reheat from frozen warm in an oven pre-heated to 200°C/400°F/Gas 6/Fan 180°C for 5 minutes.

1 x 198 g can sweetcorn, drained
2 large spring onions, quartered
1 egg
1 tbsp clear honey
50 g (2 oz) self-raising flour
2–3 tbsp sunflower oil, for frying
a pinch of salt (optional)

Whizzing the corn so that the pancakes aren't lumpy makes them much better for smaller children. It also results in a slightly thicker batter, which makes the pancakes more robust and so more suitable for finger foods. They are delicious for breakfast, lunch or tea.

Put the sweetcorn and onions in a food processor and whiz until finely chopped. Add the egg and honey, and whiz again then add the flour and a pinch of salt (optional) and pulse until combined. Transfer the batter to a jug.

Heat a little oil in a large non-stick frying pan. Drop tablespoonfuls of the batter into the pan and cook for 1½–2 minutes, until the underside is golden and bubbles are appearing on the surface of the pancakes. Flip over using a spatula and cook for a further 1–2 minutes, until golden. Cool slightly before serving. You can also make tiny pancakes by cooking teaspoonfuls of batter. Can be kept in the fridge, cooked, for 2 days. Suitable for reheating for 10–15 seconds in a microwave or in a pan over a gentle heat.

Baked Mozzarella Sticks

The key to making mozzarella sticks is to ensure a good coating of breadcrumbs, which will prevent the cheese from melting all over the baking sheet. If you see any bald patches after breadcrumbing then dip that spot back in the egg and press on some extra breadcrumbs. You can fry the sticks if you prefer: just omit the olive oil from the recipe and shallow fry over a medium heat for 2–3 minutes per side.

Pre-heat the oven to 200°C/400°F/Gas 6/Fan 180°C.

Cut the mozzarella lengthways into four; the slices should be about 1.5 cm (about ½ in) thick. Cut each slice lengthways into four to get 16 sticks (if using balls then pat off any excess water with kitchen paper).

Put the breadcrumbs in a bowl and mix in the Parmesan, paprika, and salt and pepper to taste, then stir in the oil, using a fork and making sure the oil is distributed evenly. Beat the eggs in a medium-sized bowl.

Dip 2–3 mozzarella sticks into the egg and carefully roll in the breadcrumbs. Dip in the egg again and roll in a second coat of breadcrumbs, making sure the mozzarella is well covered. Put the coated sticks on a baking sheet lined with non-stick baking parchment. Repeat with the remaining mozzarella.

Bake the sticks for 4 minutes, turn and bake for a further 3–4 minutes, until the breadcrumbs are turning golden. Don't worry if the odd bit of mozzarella melts out. Remove from the oven and let the sticks stand for 5–6 minutes, to allow the cheese to cool and firm up slightly. Meanwhile warm the tomato sauce.

Serve the sticks with pots of tomato sauce for dunking. For smaller children it may help to cut each stick into 2 or 3 pieces.

Preparation 15 minutes
Cook 8 minutes
Makes 16 sticks or about 3 portions
Suitable for freezing: put the sticks on a tray lined with cling film. Cover with more cling film and freeze for 3–4 hours, until firm. Transfer to plastic freezer bags and use within 1 month. Bake direct from frozen, increasing baking time to 10–11 minutes and turning halfway through. Suitable for reheating.

125 g (4½oz) firm mozzarella
100 g (3½ oz) dried breadcrumbs
30 g (1 oz) Parmesan, freshly grated
1 tsp paprika
4 tsp olive oil
2 eggs, beaten
salt and pepper, to season
4 tbsp tomato sauce, to serve (try Quick Tomato Sauce, p. 32, or use your favourite)

Baked Parsnip and Sweet Potato Crisps

🍲 Preparation 8 minutes
🕐 Cook 15–20 minutes
🍴 Makes 4 portions
❄ Not suitable for freezing
or reheating

1 small parsnip, peeled
½ small sweet potato, peeled
1 tbsp olive oil
a pinch of salt (optional)

TIP
The potato and parsnip cook at slightly different rates so it is easier to cook them on separate baking sheets. Watch them carefully towards the end of the cooking time.

Kids who don't always like vegetables may be fooled into eating these crisps as they are naturally slightly sweet and very delicious. And they are healthier too, as they are baked rather than fried. They would be a nice accompaniment for a Veggie Bite/Burger (see p. 24).

Pre-heat the oven to 150°C/300°F/Gas 2/Fan 130°C. Line two large baking sheets with non-stick baking parchment.

Use a small swivel peeler to peel thin strips from the parsnip. Put the strips in a bowl and toss with half of the oil. Spread out in a single layer on one of the prepared baking sheets. Do the same with the sweet potato, spreading the strips on the second baking sheet.

Bake for 10 minutes then swap the baking sheets around. Bake for a further 5 minutes then check and remove from the oven if crisp and browned at the edges. Otherwise continue cooking for a further 4–5 minutes, checking every minute, as the crisps can go brown very quickly. You may find that the parsnips cook slightly more quickly than the potato.

Transfer the cooked crisps to a bowl and sprinkle over a pinch of salt, if you like. These are best served the day they are made but can be stored in an airtight container overnight (they may soften a bit).

Cottage Cheese Dip

🍲 Preparation 5 minutes
🕐 Makes 5–6 portions
❄ Not suitable for freezing
or reheating

250 g tub cottage cheese
4 tbsp mayonnaise
2½ tbsp tomato ketchup
¼ tsp fresh lemon juice
a tiny drop of Worcestershire
    sauce (optional)

Cottage cheese is a great source of calcium, but many children don't like the texture. However, whizzing the cheese until smooth can give the base for a yummy dip.

Put all the ingredients in a food processor and whiz until smooth. Transfer to a bowl and store in the fridge until ready to use – this would make a good dipping sauce for sticks of cucumber, carrot and red pepper. If you want to prepare the vegetables in advance, wrap them in damp kitchen paper and store in the fridge to keep them fresh.

Variation: Cottage Cheese with Swirled Fruit Purée

Blend the cottage cheese with a little sugar and vanilla extract, and swirl in some shop-bought apricot purée or compote such as Bonne Maman.

Baby Baked Potatoes

Stuffed baked potatoes are usually popular with older children but are a bit unwieldy for little ones. Small new potatoes make a perfect alternative for a finger-sized version!

Pre-heat the oven to 200°C/400°F/Gas 6/Fan 180°C.

Put the potatoes into a medium bowl, drizzle over the oil and season with a little salt and pepper. Toss to coat the potatoes with the oil then transfer to a baking sheet. Bake for 30–35 minutes, until the potatoes are cooked through.

Remove the potatoes from the oven and leave to cool slightly, then cut in half and carefully scoop out some of the centre with a teaspoon. Put the scooped potato into a small bowl and add the soured cream and chives. Mash together thoroughly and season to taste with salt and pepper.

Spoon the filling into the potato skins and sprinkle over the cheese (if using). Return to the baking sheet and bake for a further 5–10 minutes, until heated through.

Suitable for reheating: the filled potatoes can be chilled overnight then reheated in a 200°C/400°F/Gas 6/Fan 180°C oven for 15–20 minutes, but they do not reheat well after they have been stuffed and baked as they get a bit dry. Not suitable for freezing.

Preparation 10 minutes
Cook 45 minutes
Makes 4 portions (older children)

8 new potatoes
1 tsp olive oil
3 tbsp soured cream or crème fraîche
1 tsp snipped chives or 1 small spring onion, finely chopped
30 g (1 oz) grated cheese (optional)
salt and pepper, to season

Vegetable Tempura

Crisp tempura batter is usually a good way to tempt sworn veggie-haters to take a taste. To keep the batter light, mix it as quickly as possible and don't worry if there are a few lumps.

Stir the dipping-sauce ingredients together until the sugar has dissolved. Divide among four small dipping bowls and set aside.

Have all of the vegetables prepared before you make the batter. You can prepare them a couple of hours in advance and keep them on a plate in the fridge, covered with a damp piece of kitchen paper and then wrapped with cling film.

Put the oil in a large, deep pan (it should not come more than halfway up the side of the pan) or deep fat fryer. Heat the oil to 190°C/375°F. Line a couple of baking sheets with a double layer of kitchen paper.

Put the flour and cornflour in a large bowl and mix together with a fork. Add the sparkling water and mix quickly with the fork – don't worry if there are a few lumps. The batter should be the consistency of single cream; if it is too thick, add an extra one or two tablespoons of water.

Drop five or six pieces of the prepared vegetables into the batter then gently put them one by one into the hot oil. Don't overcrowd the pan or the oil will get too cold and the batter will be greasy. Fry for 2–3 minutes, turning once, until puffed and crisp and turning slightly golden at the edges. Use a slotted spoon to transfer the cooked vegetables to the baking sheets and let them drain for 1–2 minutes. Meanwhile continue dipping and cooking the remainder of the vegetables. The tempura is best eaten within a few minutes of being cooked, but can be kept warm in an oven pre-heated to 120°C/250°F/Gas ½/Fan 100°C for 10–15 minutes.

Preparation 20 minutes
Cook 15–20 minutes
Makes 4 portions

½ red pepper, seeded and cut into thin strips
1 small yellow courgette (or green if unavailable), cut into ½ cm (about ¼ in) thick rounds
1 small head broccoli, broken into bite-sized florets
a handful of mangetout, trimmed
450 ml (15 fl oz) vegetable oil, for deep frying
100 g (3½ oz) flour
50 g (2 oz) cornflour
250 ml (¼ pint) sparkling water or soda water

For the dipping sauce
2 tbsp mirin
1 tbsp soy sauce
1 tbsp water
½ tsp sugar

TIP
You can also test the heat of the oil by dropping a cube of bread into the oil – if it is the correct temperature the bread should turn golden brown in around 20 seconds.

Cheese and 'Onion' Sandwich

🥣 Preparation 5 minutes
🍽 Makes 1 portion

2–3 chives, finely snipped
1 tbsp mayonnaise
1 tsp water
45 g (1¹/₂ oz) Cheddar (mild or mature, according to your child's preference), grated
2 slices bread
15 g (¹/₂ oz butter), at room temperature

Onion can be a bit strong for smaller children, but the milder taste of chives makes a standard cheese sandwich a little more interesting. Rolling the bread gives a thin sandwich that smaller children find easier to eat.

Mix the chives, mayonnaise and water together in a small bowl then add the cheese and stir to combine.

Roll the slices of bread with a rolling pin until they are about half of their original thickness. Spread one side of each slice with a little butter. Spoon the cheese filling on to one of the buttered slices and sandwich with the second slice, pressing down well. Trim off the crusts and cut into squares or triangles to serve.

Mini Vegetable Balls

The combination of the sautéed red onion and grated carrot mixed with vegetables and flavoured with Gruyère, Parmesan and balsamic vinegar with a touch of soy sauce is bound to please everyone in the family. For older children, these would make delicious burgers and a nice change from beef burgers.

Heat the oil in a frying pan and sauté the vegetables for 8 minutes. Add the thyme and garlic and cook for 2 minutes. The vegetables should be fairly dry. Add the balsamic vinegar and cook for 30 seconds–1 minute until evaporated. Turn off the heat and stir in the sugar. Leave to cool slightly.

Put the bread in a food processor and whiz into crumbs. Add the vegetables, Gruyère, two tablespoons of the Parmesan and the soy sauce, and season with pepper, then whiz until combined. Take teaspoonfuls and roll into balls. For bigger kids, take tablespoonfuls and form into burgers.

Mix the dried breadcrumbs and remaining Parmesan on a plate with a little pepper. Put the flour on a separate plate and the egg in a bowl. Toss the balls in the flour then dip in the egg and coat in the breadcrumbs.

Heat the sunflower oil in a frying pan and fry the balls for approximately 2 minutes, turning occasionally, or, for the burgers, for about 2 minutes each side. Drain on kitchen paper and cool (to warm) before serving.

Preparation 20 minutes
Cooking 2 minutes (balls), 4 minutes (burgers)
Makes 27 balls
Suitable for children under 1 year old
Suitable for freezing and reheating: freeze uncooked and cook from frozen – add 1 minute to the cooking time.

1 tbsp olive oil
1 small red onion, finely chopped
1 small carrot, peeled and finely grated
3 mushrooms, diced
1/2 small courgette, grated
3 broccoli florets, chopped into small pieces
1/4 tsp fresh thyme leaves
1 garlic clove, crushed
1 tbsp balsamic vinegar
1 slice white bread, crusts removed
30 g (1 oz) Gruyère cheese, grated
5 tbsp freshly grated Parmesan
1/2 tbsp dark soy sauce
3 tbsp dried breadcrumbs
1 1/2 tbsp flour
1 egg, beaten with a pinch of salt (omit salt for those under 1)
3–4 tbsp sunflower oil, for frying
freshly ground black pepper

Fun Fish

Apart from fish being quick to cook and a fantastic source of protein, the omega-3s in oily fish are important for boosting brainpower. Omega-3s can also revolutionize the lives of parents coping with youngsters who have dyslexia, ADHD (attention-deficit hyperactivity disorder) and dyspraxia. There is overwhelming evidence that increasing omega-3 intake can result in improved concentration, learning and behaviour. Ideally children should have two portions of oily fish a week (but not more as there are concerns over the level of toxins).

Salmon Fishcakes

🍲 Preparation 10 minutes
🕐 Cook 5 minutes
🍽 Makes 12 fishcakes
☺ Suitable for children under
1 year old
❄ Not recommended for
freezing or reheating: uncooked
mixture can be stored, covered,
in the fridge for 2–3 days.

1 x 213 g can red salmon, drained
2 slices white bread, crusts
   removed
2 spring onions, finely chopped
2 tbsp tomato ketchup
1 tsp fresh lemon juice
1 tbsp mayonnaise
2 tbsp flour
2–3 tbsp sunflower oil, for frying
salt and pepper, to season

Fishcakes are often an easy way to encourage toddlers to eat fish. You could also make these using fresh, flaked salmon.

Remove the skin and any large bones from the salmon. Whiz the bread in a food processor to make into breadcrumbs. Combine the flaked salmon, breadcrumbs, spring onions, ketchup and lemon juice in a bowl. Add the mayonnaise a teaspoon at a time until the mixture binds together (you may not need it at all). Mix well and season with salt and pepper.

   Heat the oil in a pan. Put the flour in a small bowl and season with salt and pepper. Take tablespoonfuls of the mixture and roll into balls. Roll the balls in flour, flatten in the pan with the back of a spoon or a spatula and fry for 4 to 5 minutes, turning occasionally. Blot on kitchen paper and cool slightly before serving.

Marinated Tiger Prawns with Tomato Salsa

Prawns with a tasty dip make good finger food for the whole family, and the beauty of these is they are so quick to cook.

Put the prawns in a small, flat dish and add the lime juice, coriander, soy sauce and black pepper. Chill for a minimum of 30 minutes, but no longer than 1 hour as the lime juice will start to 'cook' the prawns.

Meanwhile make the salsa. Mix together all the ingredients except the coriander and store in the fridge until needed.

Remove the prawns from the marinade and pat dry. Heat the oil in a frying pan and fry the prawns for about 90 seconds. Add one tablespoon of the marinade and allow to evaporate. Turn over the prawns and fry again for a further 90 seconds, then add another tablespoon of the marinade and allow to evaporate. Check the prawns are cooked by cutting into the fattest part of one.

When the prawns are cooked, stir the chopped coriander into the salsa and serve immediately.

⏲ Preparation 15 minutes, plus 30 minutes' marinating
🕐 Cook 3 minutes
🍽 Makes 2–3 portions

125 g (4½ oz) raw peeled tiger prawns
juice of 1 large lime
1 tsp roughly chopped fresh coriander
1 tsp dark soy sauce
freshly ground black pepper, to season
1 tbsp sunflower oil, for frying

For the tomato salsa
1 tbsp finely chopped red onion
2 tomatoes, quartered, seeded and finely diced
2 tbsp olive oil
1 tsp dark soy sauce
1 tsp rice wine vinegar
1 tsp fresh lime juice
1 tbsp chopped fresh coriander (optional)

Krispie Fish 'Fingers' with Lemon Mayo Dip

⏲ Preparation 20 minutes
🕐 Cook 3–4 minutes
🍽 Makes 6–8 portions
❄ Suitable for freezing: lay the uncooked fish fingers on a baking sheet lined with cling film. Cover with cling film and freeze for around 2 hours, until firm. Transfer to re-sealable plastic bags. Cook direct from frozen as described left (the cooking time is the same). Not suitable for reheating.

225 g (8 oz) skinless sole
   or plaice fillets
45 g (1¹/₂ oz) Rice Krispies
3 tbsp freshly grated Parmesan
¹/₄ tsp paprika
1 tsp sesame seeds (optional)
1 egg
2 tbsp flour
2–3 tbsp sunflower oil, for frying
salt and pepper, to season

For the dip
2 tbsp mayonnaise
2 tbsp thick Greek yoghurt
1 tsp fresh lemon juice
a pinch of salt, to season
   (optional)

Rice Krispies make a tasty coating for fish, and I like to make these finger-sized goujons as they cook quickly and can be easily cooked from frozen. Another good coating to try is crushed cornflakes. Simply cut the fish into strips, coat in seasoned flour, lightly beaten egg and then crushed cornflakes, and sauté until golden and cooked through.

Cut the fish into little finger-sized pieces. Cover and set aside in the fridge. Put the Rice Krispies, Parmesan and paprika in a food processor, and whiz to fine crumbs. Transfer to a plate, and stir in salt and pepper to taste and the sesame seeds (if using). Beat the egg in a bowl with a pinch of salt. Spread the flour out on a separate plate.

Toss three or four of the fish pieces in the flour then dunk in the egg and roll in the Krispie crumbs until well coated. Sit on a clean plate and continue with remaining fish. Cook immediately or freeze according to the instructions on the right.

Heat the oil in a large frying pan and add the fish fingers. Fry for 1¹/₂ –2 minutes each side, until golden and cooked through. Transfer to a plate lined with kitchen paper to cool slightly before serving.

To make the dip, mix all of the ingredients together in a small bowl. If you like you can season the dip to taste with a pinch of salt. Serve with the fish fingers.

'Moneybag' Wontons

Wontons make great finger food and are surprisingly easy to make, plus children will enjoy helping to assemble the little parcels. As you are working, keep the pile of wonton wrappers covered with damp kitchen paper and a piece of cling film to stop them drying out. You will also need a steamer basket and pan and some non-stick baking parchment.

Put one tablespoon of water in a medium pan and heat until steaming. Add the spinach, cover and cook for 1–2 minutes, until the spinach has wilted. Drain and allow to cool slightly, then squeeze out as much liquid as possible.

Transfer the spinach to a food processor, add the shelled prawns and water chestnuts, and whiz briefly, until chopped. Add the onions, ginger, mirin, sugar, oyster sauce and soy sauce, and pulse until the prawns are roughly chopped.

Lay a wonton wrapper on a chopping board and dampen the edges. Put two teaspoonfuls of the filling in the centre of the wonton and bring the corners together. Pinch just above the filling to seal. Alternatively fold over to form a triangle. Sit the wonton on a baking sheet lined with cling film, and cover with another piece of cling film. Repeat with remaining wonton wrappers and filling.

The wontons will sit, covered, in the fridge for a couple of hours. If keeping any longer follow the freezing instructions (right). To cook, line the base of a steamer basket with a circle of non-stick baking parchment (the Chinese often use lettuce leaves!) and place the wontons on top. Sit the steamer over a pot of boiling water and cover. Steam for 8 minutes, until cooked all the way through. Serve with extra soy sauce for dipping.

Preparation 25 minutes
Cook 8 minutes
Makes 12 wontons
Suitable for freezing: put the covered wontons in the freezer for 2–3 hours, until solid. Transfer to a freezer bag and store in the freezer for up to one month. Steam direct from frozen, increase steaming time to 10 minutes. Not suitable for reheating.

30 g (1 oz) baby spinach leaves, well washed
125 g (4½ oz) raw prawns, shell on
4–5 water chestnuts, quartered
2 spring onions, thinly sliced
½ tsp grated fresh root ginger
1 tsp mirin
1 tsp sugar
1 tsp oyster sauce
½ tsp dark soy sauce, plus extra for dipping
12 wonton wrappers (available from Asian supermarkets in the chilled section)

TIP
If freezing use prawns that haven't been previously frozen, or use cooked prawns.

Sweet Chilli Salmon Skewers

🍴 Preparation 5 minutes,
plus marinating
🕐 Cook 7 minutes
🍳 Makes 4 skewers or
2–3 portions
❄ Not suitable for freezing
or reheating

2 tsp sweet chilli sauce
1½ tsp mirin
½ tsp dark soy sauce
225 g (8 oz) salmon fillets,
    skin removed and cut into
    1 cm (about ½ in) cubes
You will also need 4 wooden
    skewers, soaked in water
    for 20 minutes

Oily fish, for example salmon, is a good source of omega-3 oils and should be offered a couple of times a week. Marinades, such as this delicious sweet-chilli one, can help to tempt children who may not always want to try fish.

Mix the chilli sauce, mirin and soy sauce together in a bowl. Add the salmon and toss to coat. Leave to marinate for 15–20 minutes, stirring two to three times.

Pre-heat the grill to High and line a grill pan with foil. Thread the salmon on to the skewers and sit them on the foil. Spoon over half of the marinade left in the bowl and grill the salmon for 3 minutes. Turn the skewers over, spoon over the rest of the marinade and grill for a further 3–4 minutes, until the salmon is cooked through.

Cool slightly – for smaller children it may be best to remove the salmon from the skewers before serving.

Teryaki Salmon

You can vary this recipe, depending on your child's preferences. You could perhaps make it without the sesame seeds, and for children who aren't too keen on ginger you may want to add just a little.

Toast the sesame seeds by putting them in a small frying pan over a medium heat for 2–3 minutes, stirring two or three times. Spread out on a plate and allow to cool.

Cut the salmon into 1 cm (½ in) cubes. Thread three to four cubes on to each skewer and put the skewers on a foil-lined baking sheet.

Pre-heat the grill to High. Scrape the skin from the ginger using the tip of a teaspoon. Grate the ginger finely – you need quarter of a teaspoon. Put the ginger in a bowl with the soy sauce and honey, and mix together.

Brush some of the teryaki sauce on to the salmon and grill for 2 minutes, as close to the flame as possible. Brush again with the teryaki sauce and grill for another 2 minutes. Turn the skewers over, and repeat the brushing and grilling process.

Cool the skewers slightly and serve sprinkled with the toasted sesame seeds. For smaller children it may be a good idea to remove the skewers before serving.

Preparation 5 minutes
Cook 8 minutes
Makes 6 skewers
Not suitable for freezing or reheating

1 tbsp sesame seeds
200 g (7 oz) skinless salmon fillet
a small piece of fresh root ginger
1½ tsp dark soy sauce
1 tbsp clear honey
You will also need 6 wooden skewers, soaked in water for 30 minutes

TIP
It is easier to grate ginger if you freeze it first.

Pressed Sushi

🍳 Preparation 15 minutes
🕐 Cook 15 minutes
🍥 Makes about 32 sushi
❄ Not suitable for freezing
or reheating

250 g (9 oz) sushi rice
350 ml (12 fl oz) water
3 tbsp rice wine vinegar
2 tbsp caster sugar
¼ tsp salt
4–6 thin slices smoked salmon

TIP
This is a fun dish for older
children to make.

The Japanese call this type of sushi 'oshi sushi', and it is
surprisingly easy to make. The sushi will cut more easily if
you wet the knife between each cut. Although not suitable
for freezing, it can be stored overnight in the fridge wrapped
tightly in cling film.

Put the rice in a pan with the water. Bring up to a boil, cover
the pan tightly with a lid, turn down the heat as low as possible
and cook for 15 minutes. Turn off the heat and leave to stand
for another 15 minutes.

Meanwhile warm the vinegar in a microwave for 10 seconds
or warm gently in a pan but do not boil, then stir in the sugar
and salt until dissolved. Line a 20 cm (8 in) loose-bottomed/
springform cake tin with two pieces of cling film, allowing
plenty of overhang. Lay the smoked salmon on the base of
the cake tin, overlapping the slices slightly.

Spoon the cooked rice into a large bowl and stir in the vinegar
mixture. Leave the rice to cool for 10 minutes, stirring regularly.
Spread the rice over the salmon, fold the cling film over the top
of the rice then press the rice down firmly with a potato masher.

Chill for 30 minutes. Lift out the base of the cake tin, unwrap
the cling film from the rice side and flip the sushi disc on to a
cutting board (salmon-side up). Remove cling film completely
and cut into pieces with a sharp knife. Serve with soy sauce
for dipping.

Coconut Shrimp

Coconut shrimp is a hugely popular dish in America. I'm not sure who thought of the addition of coconut originally, but the flavour seems to complement the sweetness of the prawns. I love the very light and crispy Japanese panko breadcrumbs, but if you can't find them then use ordinary dried breadcrumbs instead.

Mix the dipping sauce ingredients together in a small bowl. Divide among four smaller dipping bowls and set aside.

Pat the prawns dry with kitchen paper. Spread the flour out on a large plate. Whisk the egg and soy sauce together in a bowl. Mix the breadcrumbs and coconut together and spread out on a second plate. Dust the prawns with flour then dip in the egg and roll in the coconut breadcrumbs. Transfer to a plate or tray. The breadcrumb-coated prawns can be kept in the fridge, covered, for 2 hours before cooking.

Put some sunflower oil in a wok or deep-sided frying pan, to the depth of 1 cm (1/2 in). Heat over a medium heat, until a breadcrumb dropped into the oil sizzles and browns in around 30 seconds. Add the coated prawns and cook for 2–3 minutes each side, until golden. If the prawns are browning too quickly then lower the heat slightly. Don't overcrowd the pan – you may need to cook the prawns in two batches. Drain the cooked prawns on a couple of layers of kitchen paper and allow to cool slightly, then serve with the dipping sauce – the cocktail sauce from the Prawn Cocktail Lettuce Boats (see p. 119), would make a good alternative dipping sauce.

Preparation 20 minutes, plus any defrosting time
Cook 6 minutes
Makes 3–4 portions (recipe easily halved or doubled)
Not suitable for freezing or reheating

12 raw tiger prawns (defrosted if frozen), peeled, deveined and tails removed
2 tbsp flour
1 egg
1/2 tsp dark soy sauce
30 g (1 oz) panko breadcrumbs or dried breadcrumbs
20 g (3/4 oz) desiccated coconut
sunflower oil, for frying

For the dipping sauce
2 tbsp sweet chilli sauce
2 tsp rice wine vinegar
1 tsp mirin

Salmon Dip with Mock Melba Toast

🥣 Preparation 5 minutes (dip),
5 minutes (toast)
🕐 Cook 8 minutes (for 4 pieces
of toast)
🍽 Makes 4 portions
❄ Not suitable for freezing
or reheating

213 g can pink salmon, drained
    with large pieces of skin
    and bone removed
50 g (2 oz) full fat soft cheese
1 tbsp tomato ketchup
1 tbsp mayonnaise
1 tbsp Greek yoghurt or soured
    cream
2 tsp fresh lemon juice
4 slices bread (brown or white)
salt and pepper, to season

Tinned salmon is a good source of calcium for growing children and making it into a dip can be a good way to tempt them to eat it. I love Melba toast, but it is fiddly to prepare. This mock Melba toast is quick to make and gives slices that are thin and crisp yet robust enough still to survive dunking.

Put all the ingredients except the bread into a food processor with salt and pepper to taste. Pulse until well combined. Transfer to a bowl and chill for 1–2 hours (it will thicken slightly as it chills).

To make the toast, roll the bread with a rolling pin until thin. Cut off the crusts and toast in a toaster (cut in half if slices are too large to fit into a toaster) or under the grill for around 2 minutes, turning once, until golden and crisp. Transfer to a toast rack or prop up the toast for 1–2 minutes to help the toast crisp up then cut into fingers. Serve with the dip. The dip will keep in the fridge for 2–3 days.

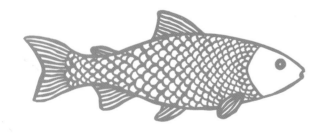

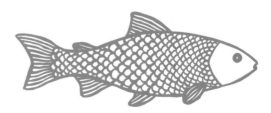

Smoked Salmon Rolls

The classic New York combination of salmon and cream cheese is beloved by adults and children alike. Toasted bagels are optional!

Put the soft cheese in a bowl and beat until softened. Mix in the lemon juice and dill or chives (if using) and season with pepper.

Lay out the salmon slices on a flat surface. You can make up the rolls in two ways: the cylinders have a solid soft-cheese centre; the pinwheels have 'stripes'. The rolls will keep, covered in the fridge, for 24 hours.

Cylinders

Put one tablespoon of the soft cheese mixture at one of the short ends of the salmon and spread out slightly. Roll the slice of salmon up tightly from the soft cheese end to form a cylinder. If possible cover and chill for 2–3 hours to allow the soft cheese to firm up. Cut into four slices.

Pinwheels

Spread one tablespoon of the soft cheese mixture over each slice of salmon. Roll up tightly from one of the short ends. If possible cover and chill for 2–3 hours to allow the soft cheese to firm up. Cut into five slices.

🍲 Preparation 10 minutes, plus chilling
🎨 Makes 4 portions
❄ Suitable for freezing: defrost overnight in the fridge.

50 g (2 oz) full fat soft cheese (reduced fat version is also fine)
½ tsp fresh lemon juice
½ tsp finely chopped fresh dill or snipped chives (optional)
4 large slices smoked salmon
salt and pepper, to season

Not suitable for children under 1 year old as salt level is too high.

Finger-licking Chicken

Chicken is popular with children and good for them too – the darker meat contains twice as much iron and zinc as the white meat, supporting a healthy immune system and aiding growth and development. It's easy to make chicken nuggets – one of the most popular finger foods for children – and you can be sure they are good quality. Chicken on the griddle is also delicious and ready in minutes. Take care, though, chicken must be cooked thoroughly to prevent possible salmonella poisoning.

Parmesan Chicken Fingers

🍽 Preparation 15 minutes
🕐 Cook 6 minutes
🍲 Makes 3–4 portions
☺ Suitable for children under 1 year old
❄ Suitable for freezing: put the uncooked, coated chicken fingers on a baking sheet lined with cling film. Cover with a second piece of cling film and freeze until firm then transfer to a freezer bag. Cook direct from frozen, adding an extra minute to the cooking time. Not suitable for reheating but good cold.

1 boneless skinless chicken
    breast (about 125 g/
    4¹/₂ oz)
1 egg white
50 g (2 oz) Parmesan, freshly
    grated
freshly ground pepper, to taste

TIP
This is a good recipe for children with wheat/gluten allergies. Leftovers can be used in the Mix 'n' Match Pasta Salad (p.117).

Children seem to love the combination of cheese and chicken and may like to help making these easy chicken fingers. You do need to make sure the chicken breast is beaten out nice and thin, so that the chicken fingers cook quickly. The chicken fingers can be served warm with ketchup or my Quick Tomato Sauce (see p. 32), and cold in sandwiches with some mayonnaise and lettuce.

Cut the chicken breast in half horizontally though the centre. Put the two pieces of chicken between two sheets of cling film and beat with a mallet or rolling pin until ¹/₂ cm (¹/₄ in) thick. Remove the cling film and cut the flattened chicken into small strips, about 5 cm (2 in) long.

Beat the egg white with a little pepper, until frothy. Spread the Parmesan out on a large plate. Dip the chicken strips in the egg white and roll in the Parmesan to coat.

Pre-heat the grill to High and line a grill pan with foil. Grill the chicken fingers for 2–3 minutes, until the cheese is golden. Turn over and cook for a further 2–3 minutes, until the chicken has cooked through. Cool slightly before serving.

Cajun Chicken Skewers with Mango Salsa

You could also try making these using sweet smoked Spanish paprika, which is available in some supermarkets.

Pre-heat the grill to High. Mix the chicken with the paprika, garlic, sunflower oil and black pepper. Thread the chicken on to eight skewers. Place the chicken on a lightly oiled baking sheet and grill for about 3–4 minutes on each side or until the chicken is cooked through.

To make the mango salsa, combine all the ingredients except the coriander and seasoning, and set aside. Just before serving, add the coriander and season well with the salt and pepper. For little ones remove the chicken from the skewers before serving.

🍲 Preparation 5 minutes
🕐 Cook 8 minutes
🍳 Makes 8 skewers or 4 portions
❄ Not suitable for freezing or reheating

250 g (9 oz) boneless skinless chicken breast, cut into strips
a pinch of paprika
1–2 garlic cloves, crushed
1 tbsp sunflower oil
freshly ground black pepper, to taste
You will also need 4 wooden skewers, soaked in water for 30 minutes

For the mango salsa
1/2 small red onion, very finely diced
1/2 ripe mango, very finely diced
1/2 tsp rice wine vinegar
juice of 1/2 lime
1 tbsp chopped fresh coriander
salt and pepper, to season

Turkey/Chicken Sliders

🍳 Preparation 15 minutes
🕐 Cook 24 minutes (assuming 3 batches)
🍥 Makes 22 sliders
❄ Suitable for freezing: put tablespoonfuls of the mixture on a baking sheet lined with cling film. Cover with more cling film and freeze until solid then transfer to a re-sealable box or freezer bag. Defrost overnight in the fridge and cook as above. Reheating is not recommended.

3 slices white bread, crusts
   removed
4 tbsp milk
1 red onion, finely chopped
1 tbsp olive oil
1 garlic clove, crushed
250 g (9 oz) chicken or turkey
   mince
2 tsp dark soy sauce
3 tbsp tomato chutney
1 tsp tomato purée
2 tbsp sunflower oil, for frying
salt and pepper, to season

A slider is a bite-sized burger. The Americans originally came up with the term and no one seems to be sure why – I can only assume it is because they slide down so easily when eaten! If you have older children, you could make these twice the size. Serve in the Baby Burger Buns (p.116).

Put the bread in a food processor and whiz to make breadcrumbs. Add the milk and leave to soak. Meanwhile, sauté the onion for 5 minutes in the olive oil until softened. Add the garlic and cook for a further minute. Transfer to a food processor and add the remaining ingredients. Season to taste and whiz for 1 minute to chop and combine.

   Heat the sunflower oil in a large frying pan. Drop the mixture by tablespoonfuls into the pan. Press down slightly using a wet teaspoon. Sauté for 2–3 minutes on each side or until golden and cooked through.

Krispie Chicken Nuggets

It will be hard to go back to shop-bought nuggets after you have tasted these. You can skip the marinating stage if you don't have time, but it does add a delicious flavour to the chicken.

Cut the chicken breasts into 1.5 cm (½ in) cubes and put in a bowl. Mix together the milk, garlic, thyme, lemon juice, ¼ tsp salt and some black pepper (the mixture will separate a little from the lemon juice but this is OK), and pour over the chicken. Cover, and marinate in the fridge for 4 hours or overnight.

Put the Rice Krispies in a food processor and whiz until reduced to fine crumbs. Add the cheeses plus salt and pepper to taste, and whiz to combine. Transfer to a large plate. Whisk the egg in a small bowl with the tablespoon of milk. Mix the flour with a little salt and pepper, and spread out on a large plate.

Remove the chicken pieces from the marinade, shaking off any excess. Toss in the seasoned flour then dip in the egg and roll in the Rice Krispie coating. Put the oil in a large non-stick pan over a medium heat. Fry the nuggets for 2–3 minutes each side, until golden and crisp. Drain on kitchen paper and cool slightly before serving.

Oven method

Pre-heat the oven to 200°C/400°F/Gas 6/Fan 180°C. Reduce the oil to two tablespoons. Add one tablespoon to the Rice Krispie crumbs with the cheese and whiz to combine evenly (you may need to stop and stir a couple of times). Grease a baking sheet with the remaining tablespoon of oil. Coat the chicken (as above) and put on the prepared baking sheet. Bake for 15 minutes, until cooked through, turning over halfway.

🍳 Preparation 20 minutes
🕐 Cook 12 minutes
🍽 Makes 4 portions
❄ Suitable for freezing: put uncooked, coated chicken on a baking sheet lined with cling film. Cover with more cling film, freeze until solid then transfer to a freezer bag. Cook direct from frozen, adding 1 minute of extra cooking time for frying and 3–4 minutes for baking. Reheating is not recommended.

200 g (7 oz) boneless skinless chicken breast
100 ml (3½ fl oz) milk, plus 1 tbsp for dipping
1 garlic clove, crushed
1 tsp fresh thyme leaves
1 tbsp fresh lemon juice
45 g (1½ oz) Rice Krispies
15 g (½ oz) mature Cheddar, finely grated
1 tbsp freshly grated Parmesan
1 egg
4 tbsp flour
3–4 tbsp sunflower oil, for frying
salt and black pepper, to season

TIP
Vary the marinades: use ½ tsp dried oregano or thyme, and add paprika, cayenne or Tabasco sauce if you like a bit of spice.

Sticky Soy Drumsticks

🥘 Preparation 5 minutes,
plus marinating
🕐 Cook 35–40 minutes
🍳 Makes 6 drumsticks
❄ Suitable for freezing and
reheating. Uncooked drumsticks
can be frozen in their marinade
in a freezer bag. Defrost the
bag overnight in the fridge
and cook as on right. Can be
reheated for 30 seconds in
a microwave only, because
otherwise they dry out too
much. However, they are also
good cold.

**6 small skinless chicken
    drumsticks
2 tbsp dark soy sauce
4 tbsp fresh orange juice
1 tsp grated fresh root ginger
1 garlic clove, crushed
2 tbsp maple syrup**

Kids tend to love drumsticks, and these are glazed with
a yummy combination of soy, ginger and maple syrup. Just
remember to hand out wipes for those sticky fingers. I prefer
skinless drumsticks to reduce the fat content, but you could
use skin-on.

Make a couple of cuts in the flesh of each drumstick and put
them in a bowl or re-sealable plastic bag. Mix together the soy
sauce, orange juice, ginger and garlic, pour over the chicken
and stir or shake to cover the chicken in the marinade. Cover
or seal and marinate in the fridge for a minimum of 2 hours
or overnight.

Pre-heat the oven to 200°C/400°F/Gas 6/Fan 180°C. Remove
the drumsticks from the marinade and sit in a small baking
dish that has been lined with foil and pour over the marinade
left in the bowl or bag. Cover the dish with foil and bake for
20 minutes.

Uncover the chicken, baste with the juices in the dish and
drizzle over the maple syrup. Bake for a further 15–20 minutes,
basting every 5 minutes, until the drumsticks are cooked
through and coated in a sticky glaze.

The sugar in the glaze can be very hot so it is a good idea
to allow the drumsticks to cool slightly before serving. Store
in the fridge for up to 2 days.

Honey Dijon Chicken Skewers

I love honey mustard, and this was the inspiration for the marinade. You can use wholegrain mustard instead if your children like spicier foods, but I find it has a little too much heat for smaller children.

Mix the honey, mustard, garlic, olive oil and lemon juice together in a small bowl. Add the chicken and toss to coat, then cover and marinate overnight in the fridge.

Pre-heat the grill to High and line a grill pan with foil. Remove the chicken from the marinade and thread on to the skewers. Lay the skewers on the foil and spoon over any marinade left in the bowl. Grill for 3–4 minutes each side, until the chicken has cooked through.

Cool slightly before serving. For smaller children remove the chicken from the skewers and cut into bite-sized chunks.

🍲 Preparation 5 minutes, plus marinating
🕐 Cook 8 minutes
🍽 Makes 4 skewers or 2 portions
❄ Suitable for freezing: you can freeze the chicken in the marinade in individual portion sizes. Defrost overnight in the fridge or for around 45 minutes at room temperature. Cook as on left. Reheating is not recommended but these are also good cold.

1 tbsp clear honey
½ tsp Dijon mustard
½ small garlic clove, crushed
1 tsp olive oil
½ tsp fresh lemon juice.
4 chicken mini-fillets (about 110 g/4 oz total weight) or 1 small boneless skinless chicken breast, sliced lengthways into 4, or into 2 cm (3/4 in) cubes
You will also need 4 wooden skewers, soaked in water for 30 minutes

Annabel's Chicken Rissoles

🍲 Preparation 20 minutes, includes 10 minutes for soaking the breadcrumbs
🕐 Cook 22 minutes
🍥 Makes 12 rissoles
❄ Suitable for freezing

175 g (6 oz) breadcrumbs, from white bread, crusts removed
1¹/₂ tbsp milk
150 g (5 oz) carrots, grated
150 g (5 oz) courgette, grated
2 tbsp sunflower oil, for frying
150 g (5 oz) onion, finely chopped
1 garlic clove, crushed
200 g (7 oz) minced chicken
1 tsp dried oregano
1 tbsp tomato ketchup
¹/₂ tbsp maple syrup
1 tsp soy sauce
¹/₂ tsp Worcestershire sauce
¹/₂ tsp balsamic vinegar
¹/₂ tsp caster sugar
salt and pepper, to season

For the coating
30 g (1 oz) flour
1 egg, beaten
3¹/₂ tbsp oil, for frying
a little salt and freshly ground black pepper

You can sneak some vegetables into these tasty chicken rissoles. It is good to make a batch and freeze them on a baking tray lined with cling film. When frozen, wrap each one individually in cling film so that you can take out just as many as you need.

Put 75 g (3 oz) of the breadcrumbs into a bowl then add the milk and leave to soak for 10 minutes. Squeeze a little of the moisture from the grated carrot and courgette.

Heat the sunflower oil in a frying pan and sauté the onion for 3 minutes, stirring occasionally. Add the garlic and cook for 30 seconds, then add the carrot and courgette, stirring for 5 minutes over a low heat. Transfer to a plate and keep cool.

Mix together the bread soaked in milk, the chicken, cooked veg and remaining ingredients, and season with a little salt and pepper.

To coat the rissoles, spread out the flour on a large plate. Beat the egg in a small bowl. Using floured hands, form the mixture into rissoles, coat in the flour, dip in the egg and then coat with the remaining breadcrumbs. Heat the oil in the frying pan and fry the rissoles for 12 minutes, turning occasionally, until golden brown.

Chicken Marinades

Marinades not only add flavour but also tenderise chicken. You can marinate strips of uncooked chicken and then freeze them so that they are ready to cook already marinaded.

Tomato Balsamic, Lemon & Thyme and Special Soy

For each marinade, mix together all the ingredients, transfer to a resealable bag or a bowl and marinate the chicken in the fridge for at least 1 hour. Season the chicken before you cook it, but don't add the seasoning to the marinade.

When you are ready to cook, pre-heat the grill to High. Line a baking sheet with foil and grill the chicken mini fillets for 3 to 4 minutes each side. Alternatively, you can cook them on a griddle.

Preparation 5–10 minutes, plus marinating
Cook 8–10 minutes
Makes 2–4 portions
Suitable for freezing. Reheating is not recommended.

For each marinade
110 g (4 oz) chicken mini-fillets or boneless skinless chicken breast, cut into four strips
4 wooden skewers, soaked in water for 30 minutes

Tomato Balsamic
3 cherry tomatoes
3 SunBlush tomatoes
2 tbsp olive oil
1/2 tbsp balsamic vinegar
1/2 tsp soft light brown sugar
1/2 tsp tomato purée

Lemon & Thyme
1/4 tsp fresh thyme leaves
1 small garlic clove, crushed
2 tbsp olive oil
2 tsp fresh lemon juice

Special Soy
1/4 tsp grated fresh root ginger
1 tsp dark soy sauce
1 tsp rice wine vinegar
1/2 tsp tomato purée
1/2 tsp fresh lemon juice
1/2 tsp soft light brown sugar
1 tbsp sunflower oil

BBQ Griddled Chicken

⏱ Preparation 5–10 minutes,
plus marinating
🕐 Cook 8–10 minutes
🍽 Makes 2–4 portions
❄ Suitable for freezing.
Reheating is not recommended.

110 g (4 oz) chicken mini-fillets
   or boneless skinless chicken
   breast, cut into four strips
4 wooden skewers, soaked
   in water for 30 minutes

For the marinade
2 tbsp tomato ketchup
1 tbsp maple syrup
¼ tsp dark soy sauce
2–3 drops Worcestershire sauce

In the summer you can cook marinated chicken on the barbecue. Personally, I prefer to use chicken on the bone for a barbecue as it remains more moist. Just make sure that the chicken is thoroughly cooked. You can always strip the flesh from the bone before serving.

Mix together all the ingredients, transfer to a resealable bag or a bowl and marinate the chicken in the fridge for at least 1 hour. Season the chicken before you cook it, but don't add the seasoning to the marinade.

When you are ready to cook, pre-heat the grill to High. Line a baking sheet with foil and grill the chicken mini fillets for 3 to 4 minutes each side. Alternatively, you can cook them on a griddle

Chicken Tikka Skewers

Mild curry flavours can be popular with children. Feel free to use a stronger curry paste – but only if your children like spicy food!

Mix together in a bowl the yoghurt, curry paste, honey and lemon juice. Add the chicken and stir to coat it in the marinade. Cover and marinate overnight in the fridge.

Pre-heat the grill to High and line a grill pan with foil. Remove the chicken from the marinade and thread on to the skewers. Lay the skewers on the foil and spoon over any marinade left in the bowl. Grill for 3–4 minutes each side, until the chicken has cooked through.

Cool slightly before serving. For smaller children remove the chicken from the skewers and cut into bite-sized chunks. Good cold too (reheating is not recommended).

🍲 Preparation 5 minutes, plus marinating
🕐 Cook 8 minutes
🍽 Makes 4 skewers or 2 portions
❄ Suitable for freezing: freeze the uncooked chicken in the marinade in individual portion sizes. Defrost overnight in the fridge or for around 45 minutes at room temperature.

2 tbsp Greek yoghurt
1 tsp korma or mild curry paste
½ tsp clear honey
½ tsp fresh lemon juice
4 chicken mini fillets or 110 g (4 oz) boneless skinless chicken breast, cut lengthways into 4 thin strips or into 4 cm (1½ in) cubes
You will also need 4 wooden skewers, soaked in water for 30 minutes

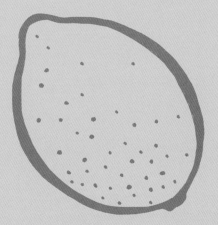

Chicken and Prawn Dumplings

🍲 Preparation 15 minutes
⏱ Cook 8 minutes
🍥 Makes 10 dumplings
❄ Suitable freezing: see method, right. Not suitable for reheating

For the filling
125 g (4½ oz) minced chicken or pork
125 g (4½ oz) peeled raw tiger prawns, deveined and roughly diced
1 large spring onion, finely chopped
¼ tsp grated fresh root ginger
1 tbsp soy sauce
1 tbsp sake
1 tsp sesame oil
2 tsp cornflour
10 wonton wrappers (available from Asian supermarkets)

For the dipping sauce
1 tbsp soy sauce
1 tbsp water
2 tsp rice wine vinegar
1 tbsp soft light brown sugar
½ tsp toasted sesame oil
¼ tsp grated fresh root ginger

My children always loved going out with us for a Chinese meal, and they particularly liked wontons and dim sum. These are not that difficult to make, and when I tested them for the first time, they were gobbled up by my three kids in less than 3 minutes.

Put the filling ingredients into a bowl and mix together.

Lay a wonton on a chopping board and dampen the edges. Put two teaspoonfuls of the filling in the centre of the wonton and bring the corners towards each other but don't actually seal together. Press the wonton gently on to the filling so it sticks to the filling and forms a round, pouch shape but is still open in the centre. Sit the wonton on a baking sheet lined with cling film, and cover with another piece of cling film. Repeat with the remaining wonton wrappers and filling.

Oil the bottom of a bamboo or stainless-steel steamer and line with greaseproof paper. Remove the dumplings from the cling film and put in the steamer, cover with a lid and place over a pan of boiling water, making sure the water does not touch the base. Steam the dumplings for 6–8 minutes until cooked.

To make the dipping sauce, stir all the ingredients together until the sugar has dissolved – if the sugar doesn't dissolve, warm gently in a pan over a low heat.

Suitable for freezing: take the uncooked clingfilm-covered wontons and freeze for 2–3 hours, until solid. Transfer to a freezer bag and store in the freezer for up to 1 month. Steam direct from frozen, increase steaming time by 5–6 minutes or until cooked through.

Chinese-glazed Chicken Wings

🍲 Preparation 5 minutes
🕐 Cook 35 minutes
🍽 Makes 3–4 portions
❄ Suitable for freezing: the uncooked chicken wings can be frozen in their marinade. Defrost thoroughly overnight in the fridge and cook as on the left.

1 garlic clove, crushed
½ tsp grated fresh root ginger
1 shallot, finely chopped
2 tbsp oyster sauce
2 tbsp dark soy sauce
1 tsp rice wine vinegar
1 tbsp clear honey
6 chicken wings, wing tips
   removed and cut in half
   at the joint

There is something quite irresistible about sweet and sticky chicken, and my easy Chinese wings are no exception. In the unlikely event of leftovers, they are also very good served cold.

Mix all of the ingredients except the chicken together in a large bowl. Add the chicken wings and toss to coat. Cover and marinate overnight, turning the chicken wings once in the marinade (you can also marinate the wings in a large, re-sealable plastic bag).

Pre-heat the oven to 200°C/400°F/Gas 6/Fan 180°C. Line a small roasting tin with foil. Tip the wings and their marinade into the tin and cover with a second sheet of foil. Roast for 20 minutes then uncover and roast for a further 10–15 minutes, or until cooked through, turning every 5 minutes, until the chicken wings are shiny and sticky.

Cool before serving – the sticky glaze can be very hot when first out of the oven. Leftovers can be kept in the fridge for up to 2 days (reheating is not recommended).

Mini Chicken Sausages

🍲 Preparation 10 minutes
🕐 Cook 6 minutes
🍥 Makes 6 sausages
☺ Suitable for children
under 1 year old
❄ Not recommended
for reheating

½ small red onion, diced
1 tbsp olive oil
2 tbsp fresh breadcrumbs,
    from ½ slice white bread,
    crusts removed
125 g (4½ oz) minced chicken
½ large eating apple, peeled
    and grated
1 tsp chopped fresh parsley
2 tbsp freshly grated Parmesan
½ chicken stock cube, dissolved
    in ½ tbsp boiling water
1 tbsp flour
3–4 tbsp sunflower oil, for frying

The combination of grated apple, sautéed red onion and Parmesan cheese gives these little sausages a lovely flavour. They are good hot or cold and just the right size for small fingers.

Sauté the onion in the olive oil for 5 minutes. Transfer to a food processor with the breadcrumbs, chicken, apple, parsley, Parmesan and stock cube, and whiz to combine.
Roll tablespoonfuls into sausage shapes and chill for 1 hour.
    Put the flour on a large plate and dust the sausages with flour. Heat the sunflower oil in a frying pan and fry the sausages for 5–6 minutes on a medium heat, turning frequently until golden.

Satay Chicken Skewers

Chicken mini-fillets are useful as they are ready portioned, but it is easy to cut up a chicken breast if that is all you have. I tend not to serve the dip to smaller children – it is so yummy that they just scoop it up and eat it neat, rather than dipping the chicken in.

Mix the ginger, garlic, lime juice, soy sauce, honey and peanut butter together in a medium bowl. Add the chicken and toss to coat. Cover and marinate for a minimum of 30 minutes, or overnight in the fridge.

Pre-heat the grill to High and line a grill pan with foil. Remove the chicken from the marinade and thread one piece on to each skewer. Lay the skewers on the foil and spoon over any marinade left in the bowl. Grill for 3–4 minutes each side, until the chicken has cooked through.

If making the satay dip, put all of the ingredients into a small pan and melt together over a low heat, stirring constantly. Bring to a boil, and cook for around 1 minute, until thickened. Remove from the heat and cool to room temperature before serving.

Serve the chicken skewers with the dip. For smaller children remove the chicken from the skewers and cut into bite-sized chunks. Tastes good cold too (reheating is not recommended).

Preparation 5 minutes, plus marinating
Cook 10 minutes (including sauce)
Makes 4 skewers or 2 portions
Suitable for freezing: you can freeze the uncooked chicken in the marinade in individual portion sizes. Defrost overnight in the fridge or for around 45 minutes at room temperature. Not recommended for reheating.

½ tsp grated fresh root ginger
½ garlic clove, crushed
2 tsp fresh lime juice
2 tsp dark soy sauce
2 tsp clear honey
4 tsp smooth peanut butter
4 chicken mini-fillets (about 110 g/4 oz total weight) or 110 g (4 oz) boneless skinless chicken breast, cut lengthways into 4 strips
You will also need 4 wooden skewers, soaked in water for 30 minutes

For the satay dip (optional)
50 g (2 oz) smooth peanut butter
3 tbsp coconut milk
2 tbsp water
2 tsp sweet chilli sauce

Apricot-Dijon Drumsticks

🍲 Preparation 5 minutes,
plus marinating
🕐 Cook 30–35 minutes
🍪 Makes 6 drumsticks
❄ Suitable for freezing and
reheating. The uncooked
drumsticks can be frozen in
the marinade in a freezer bag.
Defrost overnight in the fridge
and cook as on the right. Reheat
for 30 seconds in the microwave
only, otherwise the drumsticks
become too dry.

3 tbsp apricot jam
2 tsp Dijon mustard
1 tsp fresh lemon juice
6 skinless chicken drumsticks
    (approx. 600 g/1 lb 4 oz
    total weight) or skin-on,
    if you prefer
a little salt and freshly
    ground black pepper

Fruit and mustard may be a slightly unusual combination, but it is a delicious mix of sweet and piquant that should appeal to all the family.

Mix together the jam, mustard and lemon juice in a small bowl. Make two or three cuts in the flesh of each drumstick then put them in a large bowl or re-sealable plastic food bag. Pour over the marinade and toss to coat the drumsticks. Cover or seal and marinate in the fridge for 4 hours or overnight.

Pre-heat the oven to 200°C/400°F/Gas 6/Fan 180°C. Put the drumsticks in a baking dish lined with foil and season with salt and pepper. Pour over the marinade left in the bag, cover with foil and bake the drumsticks for 20 minutes. Uncover and turn over the drumsticks, then baste with the juices in the pan. Cook, uncovered, for a further 10–15 minutes, basting every 5 minutes with the juices in the pan, until the chicken has cooked through. Cool slightly before serving and serve warm – they are also good cold. The drumsticks will keep in the fridge for 2–3 days.

Cheat's Spring Rolls

🍽 Preparation 5 minutes
🕐 Cook 7 minutes
🍲 Makes 2 portions
❄ Not suitable for freezing
or reheating

1 tsp sunflower oil
110 g (4 oz) boneless skinless
    chicken breast, cut into
    very small strips
1 small carrot, peeled and
    coarsely grated
a handful of beansprouts
1 spring onion, thinly sliced
½ tsp dark soy sauce
1 tbsp plum sauce
2 wheat tortilla wraps

TIP
If the rolls won't stay shut
then secure with a cocktail
stick when you turn them
over to grill. Remove the
cocktail stick before serving.

Chinese spring rolls are so yummy, but as they are deep fried
they are a bit unhealthy – and tricky to do at home. So I came
up with this healthy and easy-to-make version that is just as
crispy and delicious.

Pre-heat the grill to High. Heat the oil in a wok or large frying
pan and stir fry the chicken for 2 minutes. Add the vegetables
and stir fry for a further 2 minutes, until the chicken has cooked
through and the vegetables have softened slightly (but aren't
completely soft). Stir in the soy sauce and one teaspoon of the
plum sauce, and remove from the heat.

Spread the remaining plum sauce over the two wraps
(a teaspoon on each). Divide the filling between the wraps,
spooning it on to the lower half of each wrap. Fold over the left
and right hand sides of the wrap then roll up from the bottom,
so that the filling is completely enclosed.

Carefully transfer the filled wraps to a grill pan, sitting them
seam side down. Grill for 1–1½ minutes, until the tops are crisp
and starting to brown then turn over and grill for a further
1–1½ minutes. Watch carefully as the wrap can scorch easily.
Serve immediately.

'Buffalo' Wings

Buffalo wings are very popular in America, and their name comes from the Buffalo area of New York State, where they were first served. They are usually very spicy, but this is my child-friendly version, which is still finger-lickingly good!

Pre-heat the oven to 200°C/400°F/Gas 6/Fan 180°C.

Cut off the tips of the chicken wings at the joint and discard. Cut the remaining part of the wing into two at the joint and put on a baking sheet. Season with salt, pepper and a little paprika, and bake for 40–45 minutes until golden and crisp. Alternatively, you can grill or barbecue the wings for 20–30 minutes, turning frequently.

Meanwhile put the tomato ketchup, stock, butter and chilli sauce in a small pan. Heat gently, stirring, until the butter has melted, then remove from the heat.

Transfer the cooked wings to a large bowl, pour over the sauce and toss to coat the wings. Return the wings to their baking sheet and bake for a further 5–7 minutes, until glazed, or grill/barbecue for an extra 2–3 minutes. Serve immediately.

⏱ Preparation 10 minutes
🕐 Cooking 45 minutes
🍴 Makes 3–4 portions
❄ Leftovers are unlikely, but the cooled wings will keep in the fridge for up to 2 days. They don't reheat that well but are just as tasty served cold! Not suitable for freezing.

6 whole chicken wings
4 tbsp tomato ketchup
3 tbsp vegetable stock
15 g (½ oz) butter
1–2 tsp sweet chilli sauce (or to taste)
paprika, salt and pepper, to season

Meaty Mouthfuls

I find minced meat tends to be more popular with younger children than chunks of meat, as they often don't like chewing on something hard. It is really important to include meat in your child's diet as it's a good source of iron: the most common nutritional deficiency in young children is iron deficiency, which leads to fatigue, lack of concentration and impaired mental and physical development.

Meatballs in BBQ Sauce

🍳 Preparation 20 minutes
🕐 Cook 40 minutes
🍽 Makes approx. 25 meatballs
or 4 portions
❄ Suitable for freezing: freeze
cooked meatballs in their sauce.
Defrost overnight in the fridge.
Reheat in a microwave for 30
seconds–1 minute, until piping
hot. Timing will depend on the
quantity of meatballs.
Alternatively, heat in a pan for
about 5 minutes, until piping
hot, adding a splash of water
if the sauce becomes too thick.

1 red onion, finely chopped
1 tbsp olive oil
3 fresh thyme sprigs
60 g (2 oz) fresh breadcrumbs,
    from about 3 slices bread,
    crusts removed
250 g (9 oz) minced beef
2 tbsp milk
1 tsp clear honey
salt and pepper, to season

For the BBQ sauce
100 ml (3½ fl oz) ketchup
150 ml (¼ pint) orange juice
3 tbsp clear honey
2 tbsp dark soy sauce
3 tbsp water
1 garlic clove, crushed

Meatballs are always popular with small children as they
ma tender and easy to chew. This BBQ sauce makes a delicious
change to the usual tomato sauce.

Pre-heat the oven to 200°C/400°F/Gas 6/Fan 180°C.

Sauté the onion in the oil for 5–6 minutes or until soft.
Pick the leaves from the thyme (you should have a quarter
of a teaspoon) and put in a large bowl. Add the onion,
breadcrumbs, mince, milk, honey and salt and pepper to taste.

Mix together with your hands until thoroughly combined.
Take teaspoonfuls of the mixture and roll into about 25
small balls. Put in a lightly oiled, large baking dish. Bake
for 15 minutes.

Mix together all the ingredients for the sauce, pour over
the meatballs and cook for a further 20–25 minutes, stirring
gently one or twice. Serve with rice.

Maple-ginger Sticky Sausages

Sticky sausages are a perennial favourite, and I have updated the traditional honey mixture by using maple syrup and a dash of fresh root ginger instead. These are yummy warm or cold – and don't forget wet wipes to clean fingers and faces.

Heat the oven to 200°C/400°F/Gas 6/Fan 180°C. Put the sausages into a small roasting tin or baking dish (line with foil for easier clean-up). Bake for 10 minutes. Meanwhile mix together the maple syrup, soy sauce and ginger.

Spoon any excess fat from the roasting tin/baking dish. Pour the maple mixture over the sausages and stir so that the sausages are coated in the glaze. Bake for a further 25 minutes, stirring every 10 minutes and keeping a close eye on the sausages in the last 5 minutes.

Transfer the sausages to a plate or bowl and allow to cool for around 10 minutes before serving – the glaze can be quite hot so check the temperature before serving to smaller children. Leftovers can be kept, covered, in the fridge for up to 2 days.

Preparation 5 minutes
Cook 35 minutes
Makes 24 small sausages or 4–6 portions
Not suitable for freezing or reheating (but nice cold).

24 cocktail sausages
3 tbsp maple syrup
1 tbsp dark soy sauce
1/2 tsp grated fresh root ginger

American-Italian-style Mini Meatballs

🍲 Preparation 40 minutes
🕐 Cook 30 minutes, plus 2–3 minutes for cheesey topping
🍥 Makes 8–12 portions
☺ Suitable for children under 1
❄ Suitable for freezing: cooked meatballs can be frozen. Suitable for reheating: brown the meatballs, allow to cool, then mix them with the cooled sauce. Reheat gently in a pan for 10–15 minutes or bake for 25 minutes in a pre-heated oven at 200°C/400°F/Gas 6/Fan 180°C, until piping hot.

110 g (4 oz) beef mince
110 g (4 oz) veal mince
110 g (4 oz) pork mince
30 g (1 oz) fresh white
    breadcrumbs
3 tbsp milk
a small handful of parsley
    leaves, chopped
2 tbsp freshly grated Parmesan
salt and pepper, to season
2–3 tbsp sunflower oil, for frying

For the sauce
1 tbsp olive oil
1 medium red onion, chopped
1 garlic clove, crushed
(Continued overleaf)

These are perfect for small mouths. You could substitute chicken mince for either the veal or pork or use just one type of mince.

First, make the sauce. Heat the oil in a large pan and sauté the onion for 10 minutes, until soft. Add the garlic, cook for 1 minute, then transfer half to a food processor. Add the tomatoes, purées, sugar, oregano and vegetable stock to the onions left in the pan, bring to a boil, reduce the heat and simmer for 25 minutes.

Meanwhile add the beef, veal and pork mince to the onions in the food processor. Whiz for a minute to chop everything then add the breadcrumbs, milk, parsley, Parmesan and salt and pepper to taste. Pulse until well combined. Take rounded teaspoonfuls of the meatball mixture and form into about 30 small balls. You can now either fry the meatballs or cook them in the oven.

For frying Heat the oil in a large non-stick frying pan and fry in batches of 8–10 meatballs for 2–3 minutes on each side, until golden. Drain on kitchen paper.

For oven browning Pre-heat the oven to 200°C/400°F/Gas 6/Fan 180°C. Put a lipped baking sheet in the oven when you switch it on and allow it to heat up. Put two tablespoons of sunflower oil on the hot baking sheet and add the meatballs. Bake for 20 minutes, turning halfway through. Transfer the browned meatballs to the sauce using tongs or a draining spoon.

Purée the tomato sauce until smooth, and season to taste with salt and pepper. Return to the pan and add the browned meatballs. Simmer for a further 5–10 minutes. Serve with spaghetti or in hollowed out French bread.

1 x 400 g can chopped
    tomatoes
1½ tbsp tomato purée
1 tbsp sun-dried tomato purée
1 tsp soft light brown sugar
¼ tsp dried oregano
50 ml (2 fl oz) vegetable stock

Optional cheesy topping

Transfer the cooked meatballs and sauce to a heatproof dish, sprinkle over 110 g (4 oz) grated Cheddar or mozzarella and pop under a grill pre-heated to High for 2–3 minutes, until the cheese is golden and bubbling.

'Sloppy Joe' Pittas

🍲 Preparation 5 minutes
🕐 Cook 15 minutes
🌀 Makes 2 portions
❄ Suitable for freezing and reheating. Leftover sauce can be frozen for up to 1 month. Reheat in a microwave for 1–2 minutes, or for 5 minutes in a small pan over a medium heat, until piping hot.

½ tbsp olive oil
½ small onion, finely chopped
½ medium carrot, grated
    (optional)
½ small garlic clove, crushed
110 g (4 oz) minced beef (you can also use chicken or turkey)
100 ml (3½ fl oz) passata
2 tsp tomato ketchup
2 small pittas, or 1 large pitta, halved

A Sloppy Joe sandwich is a deconstructed hamburger served in a burger bun. I prefer to serve it in a pitta bread as there is slightly less chance of the filling leaking out. Either way it is delicious – if a little messy at times!

Heat the oil in a wok or medium-sized frying pan and sauté the onion and carrot (if using) for 4 minutes, until soft. Add the garlic and mince, and continue to sauté for a further 5 minutes, until the mince is browned. Keep stirring regularly to break the mince into small pieces.

Add the passata and ketchup, and simmer briskly for 4–5 minutes, until most of the liquid has evaporated and the sauce is nice and thick. Meanwhile warm the pittas for around 1 minute and then carefully ease apart to make a pocket. Spoon the Sloppy Joe mixture into the pittas (don't over-fill) and serve warm. Any leftover sauce can be kept, covered, in the fridge for up to 2 days.

Finger-sized Mini Meatloaves

Rather than making a large meatloaf and slicing, I sometimes like to make these finger-sized ones so little eaters feel like they have something special of their own. Pop one into a Baby Burger Bun (see p. 116) for a mini-meatloaf sandwich!

Pre-heat the oven to 200°C/400°F/Gas 6/Fan 180°C.

Mix the ketchup, sugar and Worcestershire sauce together in a small bowl, and set aside (if the sugar won't dissolve, warm for 10–20 seconds in a microwave or gently for a few minutes in a pan over a low heat).

Put the breadcrumbs and milk in a large bowl and leave to soak for 5 minutes. Meanwhile, sauté the onion and garlic in the olive oil for 5 minutes. Add the onion to the breadcrumbs, along with the beef, thyme and two tablespoons of the ketchup mixture. Season to taste with salt and pepper, and mix together (for a finer texture pulse in a food processor).

Divide the mixture among 16 cups in generously oiled mini-muffin tins (approximately one tablespoon each). Brush half of the remaining ketchup mixture over the top of the meatloaves and bake for 15 minutes. Brush again with any remaining ketchup mixture and bake for a further 15 minutes. Remove from the oven and leave to stand for 10 minutes (they need standing time to firm up a bit). Run a knife around the edge of each meatloaf and ease out of the tin with a teaspoon. Serve warm or cold. Any leftovers will keep in the fridge for up to 2 days.

🍲 Preparation 15 minutes
🕐 Cook 30 minutes
🌐 Makes approximately 16 meatloaves or 5–8 portions
❄ Suitable for freezing: cooked meatballs can be frozen. Suitable for reheating, preferably for 10–15 seconds in a microwave; otherwise wrap in foil and reheat at 180°C /350°F/Gas 4/Fan 160°C for 10–15 minutes until piping hot.

5 tbsp tomato ketchup
1 tbsp soft light brown sugar
1/4 tsp Worcestershire sauce
40 g (1 1/2 oz) fresh breadcrumbs, from 2 slices bread, crusts removed
6 tbsp milk
1 small red onion, grated
1 garlic clove, crushed
2 tsp olive oil, plus extra for greasing
225 g (8 oz) minced beef
1/2 tsp chopped fresh thyme leaves or 1/4 tsp dried thyme
salt and pepper, to taste

Chinese BBQ Spare Ribs

Spare ribs are easy for children to hold and are usually very popular. Hoisin sauce is often known as 'Chinese barbecue sauce', and it is a common ingredient in Char Sui – Chinese roast pork. The marinade is also delicious for chicken wings.

🍲 Preparation 5 minutes, plus marinating
🕐 Cook 1¼ hours
🍽 Makes 4 portions
❄ Suitable for freezing: the uncooked ribs can be frozen in the marinade. Defrost overnight then bake as right. Reheating is not ideal, but you can reheat in a microwave for around a minute on High or wrapped in foil in the oven for 20 minutes at 180°C/350°/Gas 4/Fan 160°C.

6 tbsp fresh orange juice
4 tbsp tomato ketchup
3 tbsp plum sauce
1½ tbsp hoisin sauce
1½ tbsp soft light brown sugar
900 g (2 lb) small spare ribs (approx. 12)

TIP
I like to marinate the ribs overnight as it allows the flavour to penetrate, but if you don't have time you can just toss the ribs in the sauce and bake straight away.

Mix together the liquid ingredients and sugar in a large bowl or re-sealable plastic bag to make a marinade, add the spare ribs and toss to coat. Cover the bowl, or close the bag, and marinate overnight in the fridge.

Heat the oven to 180°C/350°F/Gas 4/Fan 160°C and line a small roasting tin with foil. Sit the ribs in the prepared tin and pour over the marinade from the bowl or bag. Cover the tin with a second piece of foil and bake the ribs for 30 minutes. Uncover and bake for a further 30 minutes. Turn the oven up to 200°C/400°F/Gas 6/Fan 180°C and bake for a further 10–15 minutes, turning half-way through, until the ribs are glazed and sticky.

Transfer to a plate and allow the ribs to cool slightly before serving. Check the temperature before serving – the marinade can get very hot and takes a while to cool down.

Beef Skewers with Balsamic Brown Sugar Glaze

Skewers make perfect finger food as the pieces of meat are cut into bite-sized portions and the skewer makes a great vehicle for older children to eat from. This sweet and tangy glaze works very well with beef. Smaller children, though, may find even fillet beef a little too 'chewy' – so you can always make these skewers with chicken instead.

Put the balsamic vinegar, sugar and water in a small pan over a medium heat. Bring to the boil, stirring constantly, then lower the heat and simmer for 2–3 minutes, until reduced by half and looking syrupy (the glaze will leave a light coating on the bottom of the pan if you tip it slightly).

Pour into a bowl and leave to cool for 5 minutes. Add the beef and toss to coat. Leave to marinate for 10–15 minutes. Pre-heat the grill to High and line a grill pan with foil.

Slide the beef cubes on to the skewers and sit them on the foil-lined pan. Spoon over half of the marinade left in the bowl and grill for 3–4 minutes. Turn the skewers over, spoon on the remaining marinade and grill for a further 3–4 minutes, until the beef has cooked through.

Transfer the skewers to a plate and spoon over any juices sitting on the foil. Cool slightly before serving. For smaller children it may be better to remove the beef from the skewers before serving. Any leftovers will keep, covered, in the fridge for up to 2 days.

Preparation 5 minutes, plus 15 minutes' marinating
Cook 8 minutes
Makes 4 skewers or 2 portions
Not suitable for freezing. Suitable for reheating in a microwave for 1 minute (remove skewers first).

2 tbsp balsamic vinegar
1½ tbsp soft light brown sugar
1 tbsp water
150 g (5 oz) fillet or sirloin steak, cut into 1 cm (½ in) cubes
You will also need 4 wooden skewers, soaked in water for 20 minutes

TIP
Don't be tempted to marinate the meat for too long – the vinegar is acidic and will break down the meat proteins quickly, which means the meat will turn mushy.

Mini Bacon and Egg Tarts

⏲ Preparation 25 minutes
🕐 Cook 15–17 minutes
🍥 Makes 12 tarts
❄ Suitable for freezing: cooked tarts can be frozen; defrost overnight in fridge. Suitable for reheating in a microwave for about 10 seconds or in an oven pre-heated to 180°C/350°F / Gas 4/Fan 160°C for 10 minutes.

200 g (7 oz) ready-made shortcrust pastry
50 g (2 oz) thinly sliced pancetta
1 tsp olive oil
5 tbsp milk
1 tbsp cream (or use 6 tbsp milk)
1 egg, plus 1 extra yolk
pepper, to season

Kids tend to love things with bacon, and these mini tarts – manageable for small hands – are no exception. Serve them warm with salad and also cold for lunchboxes or picnics. I like to use Italian pancetta instead of ordinary bacon as it is wafer thin and perfect for tiny tarts.

Roll out the pastry to 2 mm (1/16 in) thickness and cut out pastry cases using a 6 cm (2¼ in) round cutter. Gather up and re-roll pastry trimmings and continue to cut until you have 12 pastry circles. Gently ease the pastry circles into the cups of mini-muffin tins. Chill for 15 minutes.

Meanwhile, pre-heat the oven to 200°C/400°F/Gas 6/Fan 180°C.

Cut the pancetta into small pieces and sauté in the oil for 5–6 minutes, until crisp. Drain briefly on kitchen paper and divide the pancetta among the pastry cups. Whisk together the milk, cream/extra milk, egg and egg yolk and season with a little pepper (no salt as the pancetta is salty enough). Pour the egg mixture into the pastry cups, filling almost to the top.

Bake for 15–17 minutes until slightly puffed and golden around the edges. Remove from the oven and allow to stand for 5–10 minutes before removing the tarts from the tins (run a sharp knife around the edge of each tart to help release them). Serve warm or refrigerate as soon as cool. Leftovers can be kept in the fridge for up to 2 days.

Beefy Sausage Rolls

Sausage rolls make great picnic and party finger food as they are ready-wrapped in pastry. To add a slight twist I like to use beef, but minced pork would also be good.

Put the oil in a small frying pan, add the onion and sauté for 5 minutes, until soft. Stir in the thyme and set aside. Put the bread in a food processor and whiz to crumbs. Add the onion, beef, chutney and Parmesan plus salt and pepper, and whiz again to combine.

Pre-heat the oven to 200°C/400°F/Gas 6/Fan 180°C.

Roll out the pastry into two rectangles 12 cm x 18 cm (5 in x 7 in) and about 2 mm (1/16 in) thick. Halve the meat mixture and roll into two sausages each 18 cm (7 in) long. Put one in the centre of each piece of pastry and brush the edges of the pastry with egg. Fold the edges over to enclose the meat. Cut each roll into four with a sharp knife (wipe knife between each cut) and put the rolls on to a baking sheet, seam side down. Brush the rolls with egg and cut two small slits in the top of each roll.

Bake the rolls for 16–18 minutes, until the pastry is golden brown. Use a fish slice or palette knife to transfer the rolls to a wire rack to cool. Most delicious when served warm, but can be served cold.

🍲 Preparation 20 minutes
🕐 Cook 23 minutes
🍽 Makes 8 sausage rolls
❄ The sausage rolls will keep in the fridge for up to 2 days. Suitable for reheating at 100°C/215°F/Gas1/4/Fan 80°C for 8–10 minutes. Suitable for freezing, unbaked, for up to 1 month. Defrost overnight in the fridge and bake as on the left.

1/2 tbsp olive oil
1/2 small red onion, chopped
1/4 tsp fresh thyme leaves
1 slice bread, crusts removed
110 g (4 oz) minced beef
1 1/2 tbsp tomato chutney
2 tbsp freshly grated Parmesan
225 g (8 oz) ready-made shortcrust pastry
1 egg, beaten with a pinch of salt
salt and pepper, to season

Minty Lamb Koftas

⏲ Preparation 20 minutes
🕐 Cook 8–10 minutes
🍽 Makes 8 koftas
❄ Leftovers will keep for up to
2 days in the fridge. Suitable for
reheating (skewers removed).
Reheat in a microwave for 20–
30 seconds per kofta; otherwise
wrap meat in foil and bake at
180°C/350°F/Gas 4/Fan 160°C
for 15 minutes, or until piping
hot. Not suitable for freezing.

1 small red onion, finely chopped
1 tbsp olive oil
1 garlic clove, crushed
½ tsp ground cumin
225 (8 oz) minced lamb
20 g (¾ oz) fresh breadcrumbs,
    from 1 slice bread, crusts
    removed
2 tsp chopped fresh mint leaves
1 tsp clear honey
1 egg yolk
salt and pepper, to season
You will also need 8 wooden
    skewers, soaked in warm
    water for 30 minutes

Children love to eat things on sticks, and sometimes I have called these 'lamb lollies' to increase the appeal. However, the koftas are also good stuffed into pittas or wraps (remove the skewer first) or even for making into slightly larger lamb burgers. Try them with my Minty Yoghurt Dressing (see p. 38).

Sauté the onion in the oil for 5–6 minutes, until soft. Add the garlic and cumin, and cook for an extra minute, then transfer to a bowl. Add the remaining ingredients, season to taste with salt and pepper, and mix thoroughly. For a finer texture pulse everything in a food processor.

Divide the mixture into eight and form into balls. Thread a skewer through each ball and use your hand firmly to form each ball into a sausage shape on the skewer. If possible chill the koftas for 1–2 hours.

Pre-heat the grill to High. Grill the koftas for 8–10 minutes, turning halfway, until cooked through. Cool slightly before serving and remove the skewers for smaller children.

Simply Snacks

When children come home from nursery or school, they are usually starving, so it's a good idea to have some healthy snacks ready on the table so that they don't just grab a bag of crisps and a chocolate biscuit. Simple things can make all the difference. Whole fruit in a bowl tends to go uneaten, but it will be much more appealing if you spend a few minutes cutting it up and arranging it on a plate, or threading bite-sized pieces on to a straw.

Basic Bread Dough – and three ways to use it

Dissolve the yeast and sugar in a small bowl using four tablespoons of the water. Leave to stand for 5 minutes – it should start to turn frothy.

Mix the flour and salt in a large bowl then add the yeast liquid, oil and remaining water. Mix to a soft dough, adding one or two teaspoons of extra water if the dough is too dry.

Turn the dough on to a lightly floured surface and knead for around 10 minutes, until the dough feels smooth and springy. Put the dough in a large, lightly oiled bowl and cover with a clean, damp cloth. Leave to rise in a warm place for 45 minutes–1 hour, until risen and doubled in size.

Turn out the dough on to a floured surface and knead for 1 minute, then use for one of the three recipes that follow.

Preparation 20 minutes, plus rising

7 g sachet fast-action yeast
1 tsp sugar
150 ml (1/4 pint) hand-hot water
225 g (8 oz) white bread flour
   (or half white, half
   wholemeal)
1/4 tsp salt (omit for under
   1 year)
1 tbsp olive oil,

Cheesy Breadsticks

Pre-heat the oven to 150°C/300°F/Gas 2/Fan 130°C.

Divide the dough into 20 equal pieces (17 g/1/2 oz each) and keep covered with a damp cloth. Take one piece and form it into a sausage shape, then roll out to a stick approximately 18 cm (7 in) long and about the thickness of a little finger. Transfer to lightly oiled baking sheets and cover with cling film while you shape the other breadsticks. Allow 2.5 cm (1 in) space between each breadstick. Brush the breadsticks with beaten egg and sprinkle over the cheese. Bake for 18–20 minutes for soft breadsticks or 30–35 minutes for crisp. Cool on a wire rack. Soft breadsticks will keep in an airtight container for 1 day, crisp for 5 days.

Preparation 45 minutes, plus rising
Cook 18–35 minutes
Makes 20 breadsticks
Suitable for children under 1
Suitable for freezing: the breadsticks can be frozen after baking.

1 quantity Basic Bread Dough
olive oil, for greasing
1 egg, beaten
6 tbsp freshly grated Parmesan

Preparation 30 minutes, plus rising
Cook 12–14 minutes
Makes 12 buns
Suitable for freezing after baking. Defrost for 1 hour at room temperature then reheat for 10 minutes in an oven pre-heated to 100°C/225°F/Gas ¼/Fan 90°C.

1 quantity Basic Bread Dough
olive oil, for greasing
1 egg, beaten
1 tsp sesame seeds

Baby Burger Buns

Pre-heat the oven to 200°C/400°F/Gas 6/Fan 180°C. Divide the dough into 12 equal pieces (30 g/1 oz each) and form into balls. Transfer to a lightly oiled baking sheet and cover with a damp cloth. Leave to rise for 10–15 minutes, until doubled in size.

Brush the tops with a little egg and sprinkle on some sesame seeds. Bake for 12–14 minutes, until golden and the base of the rolls sound hollow when tapped. Cool on a wire rack.

The bread dough can be frozen after shaping into balls. Freeze on clingfilm-lined baking sheets and when firm transfer to bags. To defrost, put as many rolls as you want to bake on to lightly greased baking sheets, covered with cling film, and leave in a warm place for 2–3 hours, until doubled in size. Brush with egg, sprinkle with sesame seeds and bake as above.

Preparation 30 minutes, plus rising
Cook 10–12 minutes
Makes 6 mini pizzas
Not suitable for reheating.

1 quantity Basic Bread Dough
olive oil, for greasing
1 tbsp tomato sauce, per pizza
30 g (1 oz) mozzarella, grated, per pizza
toppings of your choice (e.g. ham, sliced mushrooms, pepperoni, sliced peppers)

Mini Pizzas

Pre-heat the oven to 200°C/400°F/Gas 6/Fan 180°C.

Divide the dough into six portions (approximately 60 g/2 oz each). Roll out each portion to a circle about 12 cm (5 in) diameter and transfer to lightly oiled baking sheets. Spread over the tomato sauce and sprinkle over the cheese, then add any toppings. Bake for 10–12 minutes, until the cheese is bubbling and golden, and the base is crisp.

Suitable for freezing: the uncooked dough can be frozen after it is divided into six pieces. Freeze on cling-film-lined baking sheets and when firm transfer to freezer bags. Defrost on baking sheets, covered with cling film, for 1½–2 hours at room temperature then roll out pizza bases and continue as above.

Mix 'n' Match Pasta Salad with Mild Mayo

Toddlers can be notoriously picky eaters but getting them involved in the 'preparation' of their meal can help to catch their attention and also make them feel as if they have some element of choice in the matter. Put the pasta on your toddler's plate and give a selection of add-in ingredients in small bowls so that your child can pick out and add in what they like. The mild mayo can be used as a dressing, but I often give it as a dip in a separate bowl as it can make the salad a little slippery for small fingers.

Cook the pasta according to packet instructions. Drain, rinse well with cold water and leave to drain for 5 minutes. Mix together the mayonnaise, water and lemon juice and season to taste with salt and pepper. **(Continued overleaf)**

🍲 Preparation 10–15 minutes
🕐 Cook 12 minutes
🍽 Makes 1 portion (easily doubled)
☺ Suitable for children under 1 year old

30 g (1 oz) large pasta shapes, such as bows (farfalle), spirals (fusilli) or corkscrews (cavatappi)
2 tbsp mayonnaise
2 tsp water
¼ tsp fresh lemon juice
salt and pepper, to season

Protein add-ins
1 large slice ham, cut into strips
30 g (1 oz) thinly sliced roast beef, cut into small strips
30 g (1 oz) Cheddar, cut into matchsticks
30 g (1 oz) fresh mozzarella, cut into small cubes
30 g (1 oz) cooked chicken, torn into small strips
3–4 cold cooked Parmesan Chicken Fingers (see p. 72)
omlette strips *(see overleaf)*

Salad add-ins

3 cherry tomatoes, quartered

¼ small red, yellow or orange pepper, cut into matchsticks

2.5 cm (1 in) piece cucumber, peeled, seeded and cut into thin half moons

2–3 tbsp canned sweetcorn

¼ apple, peeled, cored and cut into thin slices

1 quantity Grilled Vegetable Skewers (see p. 36), removed from skewer, or 45 g (1½ oz) grilled vegetables from a delicatessen

½ medium carrot, cut into matchsticks

a small handful of blanched broccoli florets

30 g (1 oz) bite-sized blanched green beans

4 pitted olives, quartered

a handful of beansprouts

a small handful shredded red cabbage

TIP
Cutting the vegetables into matchsticks encourages babies to bite and chew, but please make sure that your child is supervised at all times when eating.

Put the pasta on your child's plate and offer one or two protein add-ins and two or three salad add-ins (according to appetite) from the lists that follow, in separate bowls to choose from. Once your toddler has assembled their salad, toss in the dressing or offer it as a dip. Leftover dressing and salad items will keep for 1–2 days in the fridge, tightly covered.

Omelette Strips

Whisk 1 egg with 1 tbsp milk and salt and pepper to taste. Melt a knob of butter in a 20 cm (8 in) frying pan and add the egg. Swirl around the pan to make a thin omelette then cook for around 3 minutes, until set. Slide on to a plate and cut into strips.

Lettuce Boats

Small lettuce leaves are custom made for yummy fillings. They are easy to pick up and a fun alternative to a sandwich or roll.

Prawn Cocktail
The prawn filling is also delicious in a wrap, with a handful of shredded iceberg or cos lettuce.

Put the mayonnaise, ketchup, sweet chilli sauce (if using) and lemon juice for the sauce in a bowl, mix together and season to taste with salt and pepper. Add the prawns and toss to coat in the dressing. Divide the prawn cocktail among the four lettuce leaves. Thread a cocktail stick through each of the lemon slices and secure one in each boat as a sail.

Chicken and Mango
You could substitute a quarter of a teaspoon of chopped fresh coriander for the mint, if you like.

Mix together the yoghurt, water, curry paste and honey in a bowl, and season to taste with salt and pepper. Add the chicken and mango and toss to coat in the dressing. Spoon the salad into the lettuce leaves and sprinkle over the chopped mint (if using).

Each lettuce boat variation
Preparation 5 minutes
Makes 4 boats or 2 portions

Prawn Cocktail
110 g (4 oz) small cooked peeled prawns
4 Little Gem lettuce leaves
4 thin slices lemon, to decorate
4 cocktail sticks, to decorate

For the cocktail sauce
2 tbsp mayonnaise
2 tsp tomato ketchup
1/2 tsp sweet chilli sauce (optional)
1/4 tsp fresh lemon juice
salt and pepper, to season

Chicken & Mango
2 tbsp thick Greek yoghurt
1/2 tsp water
1/4 tsp korma curry paste (or to taste)
1/4 tsp clear honey
50 g (2 oz) cooked chicken, diced
45 g (1 1/2 oz) ripe mango flesh, diced
4 Little Gem lettuce leaves
2 small fresh mint leaves, chopped (optional)
salt and pepper, to season

Prosciutto and Taleggio Panini

🍲 Preparation 5 minutes
🕐 Cook 6 minutes
🍽 Makes 1 portion
❄ Not suitable for freezing or reheating

1 hot-dog bun, split down
   the side
1 slice prosciutto or Parma ham
45 g (1½ oz) taleggio, orange
   rind removed and sliced thinly
olive oil, for greasing

Hot-dog buns are just right for baby panini, and the deliciously creamy Taleggio cheese in this filling (which I first ate on a mountainside in Italy) melts beautifully. You could always use fontina or even mozzarella instead.

Pre-heat either a ridged griddle pan, heavy-based frying pan or panini press. Lay the prosciutto on the base of the hot-dog bun, folding it in to fit. Sit the cheese on top of the prosciutto and sandwich with the top half of the bun, pressing down well.

Grease the pan with a little olive oil and sit the filled bun, top-side down, in the hot pan. Press down firmly with a fish slice and cook for 2 minutes, until the top of the bun is crisp and golden. Carefully turn the bun over and cook for a further 2–3 minutes, until the base of the bun is crisp and the cheese has melted.

Transfer to a plate and allow to cool slightly. Cut in half or into quarters to serve.

Tuna Muffin Melts

Preparation 5 minutes
Cook 5 minutes
Makes 2–4 portions (recipe easily halved)
Not suitable for freezing or reheating

1 x 170g can tuna, drained
1 spring onion, finely chopped
2 tbsp Greek yoghurt
2 tbsp tomato ketchup
1/4 tsp fresh lemon juice
2 drops Worcestershire sauce (optional)
2 muffins, split in half
40 g (1 1/2 oz) Cheddar, grated
salt and pepper, to season

Halved and toasted muffins are an ideal size for smaller children to pick up and eat. Don't be put off if the tuna filling makes more than you need – it keeps, covered, in the fridge for 2–3 days and also makes a good sandwich or quesadilla filling. For a quesadilla, spread half of the tuna mix over a wheat tortilla wrap, scatter over half the cheese and top with a second wrap then dry fry or grill for around 2 minutes each side, until crisp.

Pre-heat the grill to High.

Put the tuna and spring onion in a bowl and stir in the yoghurt, ketchup, lemon juice and Worcestershire sauce (if using). Season to taste with salt and pepper.

Lightly toast the muffins then pile the tuna mix on to the cut sides. Scatter over the cheese and grill for 1–2 minutes, until the cheese has melted. Cool slightly then serve cut in half or into quarters.

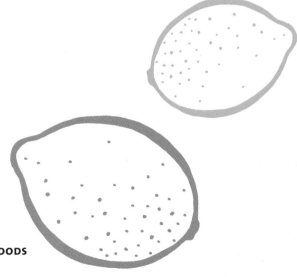

Salad Lollipops

Salad lollipops make a nice change to a sandwich in a lunchbox. It's best to remove the cocktail sticks for younger children. Or use thin drinking straws instead to secure the salad.

Cheese and Pineapple

For a fun party presentation you spear the cocktail sticks into the skin of a halved grapefruit to look like a hedgehog.

Thread a cube of cheese and a cube of pineapple on to each cocktail stick. Top with a halved cherry tomato, if using.

Tomato and Mozzarella

If making these for a lunchbox it is best to scrape the seeds out of the halved tomatoes to prevent the lollipops becoming soggy, or use whole cherry tomatoes.

Season the mozzarella with salt and pepper to taste. Thread half of a cherry tomato on to a cocktail stick, followed by a piece of mozzarella and another tomato half. Finish with a basil leaf (if using). This is good served with my Balsamic Dip (see p. 126).

Each salad lollipop variation
Preparation 10 minutes
Makes 8 lollipops or 2 portions

Cheese & Pineapple
50 g (2 oz) mild Cheddar or Red Leicester, cut into 12 cubes approx. 1.5 cm (½ in) each
6 cubes canned pineapple, drained and cut in half
6 cherry tomatoes, halved (optional)
You will also need 12 cocktail sticks

Tomato & Mozzarella
4 small mozzarella balls (bocconcini), halved, or 50 g (2 oz) fresh mozzarella, cut into 8 cubes approx. 1 cm (½ in) each
8 cherry tomatoes, halved
8 small fresh basil leaves (optional)
salt and pepper, to season
Balsamic Dip, to serve (optional)
You will also need 8 cocktail sticks

Prosciutto & Melon
¼ galia or canteloup melon, seeded and rind removed
4 slices prosciutto or Parma ham (or 4 slices wafer-thin ham)

pepper, to season
Balsamic Dip (see below),
   to serve (optional)
You will also need 8 cocktail
   sticks

Balsamic Dip
🍽 Preparation 5 minutes
🍲 Makes 2 portions

1 tbsp olive oil
1 tsp balsamic vinegar
½ tsp clear honey (or to taste)
salt and pepper, to season

Prosciutto and Melon

Cut eight cubes (each about 1.5 cm/½ in) from the melon.
Cut the prosciutto in half lengthways and slightly fold in the
long edges of each piece to give neat strips. Wrap one strip
of prosciutto around a melon cube and thread on to a cocktail
stick. Repeat with the remaining prosciutto and melon. Season
to taste with pepper. This is nice served with my Balsamic Dip.

Balsamic Dip

Whisk together the ingredients and season to taste with salt
and pepper. Serve in small bowls.

Ham and Cheese Quesadilla

Ham and cheese toasted sandwiches are perennially popular – using a tortilla wrap makes a thin, crisp sandwich that will appeal to all ages.

Pre-heat a heavy frying pan (no need to grease) or heat the grill to High.

Cut the wrap in half. Sprinkle half of the cheese on one piece of the wrap then sit the ham on top. Sprinkle over the remaining cheese and sandwich with the second piece of wrap.

Press down slightly then cook in the frying pan for 1½–2 minutes, until the base is brown and crisp. Flip over using a spatula and cook for a further 1½–2 minutes, until the cheese has melted. If you prefer, you can also grill the quesadilla for 1½–2 minutes each side.

Transfer to a plate and cool slightly before cutting into triangles or fingers to serve.

🍲 Preparation 5 minutes
🕐 Cook 5 minutes
🍥 Makes 1 portion (recipe easily doubled)
❄ Not suitable for reheating or freezing

1 soft wheat tortilla
30 g (1 oz) Cheddar, grated
1–2 thin slices ham

Chicken Fajitas with Mild Salsa

🍲 Preparation 20 minutes
🕐 Cook 7 minutes
🍥 Makes 2 portions
❄ Not suitable for freezing

2 tsp tomato ketchup
1 tsp balsamic vinegar
1 tsp water
½ tsp brown sugar
a pinch of dried oregano
2 drops Tabasco sauce (optional)
1 tsp sunflower oil
1 boneless skinless chicken
　　breast, sliced into thin strips
1 medium red onion, thinly
　　sliced
¼ small red pepper, seeded
　　and thinly sliced
¼ small yellow pepper,
　　seeded and thinly sliced
2 flour tortillas
2 tbsp mild salsa (see below)
4 tsp soured cream
1 tbsp guacamole (optional)

For the mild salsa
1 large tomato, skinned,
　　seeded and diced
1 spring onion, thinly sliced
2 tsp chopped fresh coriander
　　(or to taste)
1 tsp fresh lime juice
salt and pepper, to season

A lot of Mexican food is street food so has evolved to be eaten with the hands and makes ideal finger food. If your child doesn't like peppers just substitute with a little extra chicken. Any leftover filling will keep, covered, in the fridge for up to 2 days. Reheat for 1 minute in a microwave or in the oven in a foil package for 10 minutes at 200°C/400°F/ Gas 6/Fan 180°C until piping hot.

To make the salsa, mix all of the ingredients together in a small bowl and season to taste with salt and pepper. Cover and chill until needed – it will keep for up to 2 days in the fridge. Alternatively, use a mild shop-bought salsa.

For the fajita filling, mix together the ketchup, balsamic vinegar, water, sugar, oregano and Tabasco (if using) in a small bowl and set aside.

Heat the oil in a large pan or wok and stir fry the chicken for 2 minutes. Add the vegetables and stir fry for a further 3–4 minutes, until the chicken has cooked through and the vegetables have softened slightly. Add the ketchup mixture and cook, stirring, for a further 1 minute. Then remove from the heat.

Warm the tortillas for 10–15 seconds in a microwave, or for 1 minute each side in a dry frying pan. Spoon the fajita filling down the centre of the wrap and spoon over the salsa plus the soured cream and guacamole (if using). Roll up and serve immediately.

Sweet Treats

Well, of course, the best sweet finger food has to be fresh fruit – whether it's peeled clementines, pineapple chunks or strawberries threaded on to a skewer or wedges of peeled mango or melon. If your child isn't keen on fresh fruit you can always purée and freeze it in ice-lolly moulds. I do think, though, that children need treats occasionally – so as well as wholesome baking like courgette, orange and spice muffins and oat and raisin biscuits, I have included recipes for brownies and mini jam tarts. After all you are only a child once!

Apricot and White Chocolate Cereal Bars

🍲 Preparation 10 minutes
🕐 Cook 2 minutes
🍰 Makes 16 bars

150 g (5 oz) rolled oats
50 g (2 oz) Rice Krispies
50 g (2 oz) dried apricots,
  chopped
50 g (2 oz) pecans, chopped
  (optional)
100 g (3½ oz) butter
85 g (3 oz) golden syrup
75 g (2½ oz) white chocolate,
  broken into pieces
a pinch of salt

These chewy bars taste delicious and don't need any baking. Children enjoy making them, as they are very quick and easy to prepare.

Combine the oats, Rice Krispies, apricots and pecans in a mixing bowl. Put the butter, golden syrup, white chocolate and a pinch of salt in a large saucepan and heat gently, stirring occasionally, until melded together. Stir the oat and Rice Krispie mixture into the melted chocolae mixture until well coated.

Press the mixture into a shallow 28 cm x 18 cm (11 in x 7 in) tin lined with non-stick baking parchment using a potato masher. Place in the fridge to set, then cut into bars.

Carrot, Coconut and Pineapple Muffins

Carrot and pineapple together make deliciously moist muffins. As they have a high fruit content, these muffins are best stored in the freezer.

Pre-heat the oven to 180°C/350°F/Gas 4/Fan 160°C. Line two mini-muffin tins with paper cases (or eight holes of a regular muffin tin).

Mix together the flour, baking powder, bicarbonate of soda, cinnamon and salt in a bowl. In a separate bowl mix together the melted butter, vanilla, egg, carrot, pineapple and juice, coconut and sugar. Mix the wet ingredients into the dry ones, along with the raisins.

Spoon the mixture into the paper cases (three-quarters full) and bake for 12–14 minutes (for mini-muffins) or 20 minutes (for larger muffins), until risen and firm to the touch. Cool on a wire rack.

🖐 Preparation 15 minutes
🕐 Cook 14 minutes (mini)/
20 minutes (regular)
🍥 Makes 24 mini/8 regular muffins
❄ Suitable for freezing: freeze baked muffins in a re-sealable box or freezer bag. Defrost at room temperature for 30–45 minutes (mini) or 2 hours (regular).

150 g (5 oz) wholemeal flour or 75 g (2½ oz) wholemeal flour and 75 g (2½ oz) plain flour
1 tsp baking powder
½ tsp bicarbonate of soda
½ tsp ground cinnamon
¼ tsp salt
85 g (3 oz) butter, melted
1 tsp vanilla extract
1 egg
1 medium carrot, finely grated
60 g (2¼ oz) drained canned crushed pineapple
1 tbsp pineapple juice (from the can)
30 g (1 oz) desiccated coconut
100 g (3½ oz) soft light brown sugar
50 g (2 oz) raisins (chopped for smaller children)

Yoghurt Orange and Lemon Mini Cupcakes

🍲 Preparation 15 minutes
🕐 Cook 20 minutes
🍰 Makes approx. 18 mini cupcakes
☺ Suitable for children under 1 year old
❄ Suitable for freezing: un-iced cupcakes can be frozen in a re-sealable box or freezer bag.

50 g (2 oz) butter
100 g (3¹/₂ oz) caster sugar
1 egg, at room temperature
zest of ¹/₂ small lemon
zest of ¹/₂ lime
¹/₂ tsp orange zest
125 g (4¹/₂ oz) self-raising flour
50 ml (2 fl oz) natural yoghurt
   (not low fat)

For the icing
225 g (8 oz) icing sugar
1 tbsp fresh orange juice
1 tbsp fresh lime juice

These cute cupcakes are manageable mini mouthfuls for little ones. Adding some yoghurt and citrus fruit keeps them lovely and moist and gives them a deliciously refreshing flavour. They would be great for birthday parties.

Pre-heat the oven to 180°C/350°F/Gas 4/Fan 160°C and line a mini-muffin tin with paper cases.

Cream the butter and sugar until pale and fluffy. Gradually add the egg, beating well between additions. Stir in the zests. Sift over the flour and fold in well. Stir in the yoghurt. Divide the mixture among the mini-muffin cases and bake for 18–20 minutes until risen, lightly golden brown and firm to the touch. Cool in the tins for 5 minutes then transfer to a wire rack and cool completely.

Meanwhile, to make the icing: sift the icing sugar into a bowl. Make a well in the middle and stir in the juices and beat well. Spoon the icing on to the cooled cupcakes and allow to set for up to 30 minutes. Store in an airtight container for up to 5 days.

Ginger Snaps

Children are very fond of crisp ginger biscuits, and these little ginger snaps fit the bill perfectly. Dipping the teaspoon in water when scooping the dough will help to give you beautifully round biscuits. These are extremely yummy and so easy to prepare.

Pre-heat the oven to 150°C/300°F/Gas 2/Fan 130°C.

Beat the butter, sugar, egg and syrup together in a large bowl until fluffy and slightly paler in colour. Sift over the dry ingredients and mix to form a soft dough.

Dip a round measuring teaspoon in a glass of water and scoop up a slightly rounded teaspoon of the dough, then drop it on to a baking sheet lined with non-stick baking parchment. Continue dipping the teaspoon and scooping the remaining dough, leaving 5–6 cm (about 2 in) between each mound of dough as the biscuits will spread. You may need to bake the biscuits in batches.

Bake the biscuits for 14–16 minutes, until light brown around the edges. Remove from the oven and leave to cool for 5 minutes then use a palette knife or fish slice to transfer the biscuits to a wire rack. The biscuits will continue to crisp up as they cool.

Store in an airtight container.

🍳 Preparation 20 minutes
🕐 Cook 16 minutes
🍪 Makes approx. 28 ginger snaps
❄ Suitable for freezing: the cooked and cooled biscuits can be frozen for up to 1 month.

50 g (2 oz) butter, softened
100 g (3½ oz) soft light brown sugar
1 egg yolk
2 tbsp golden syrup
100 g (3½ oz) plain flour
2 tsp ground ginger
¼ tsp bicarbonate of soda
a pinch of salt (optional)

TIP
Bake for 2–3 minutes less for a chewier biscuit.

Courgette, Orange and Spice Muffins

🖐 Preparation 15 minutes
🕐 Cook 14 minutes (mini)/
25 minutes (regular)
🍩 Makes 24 mini/12 regular
muffins
☺ Suitable for children under
1 year old
❄ Suitable for freezing. Defrost
for 1 hour at room temperature.

140 g (5 oz) wholemeal flour
1/2 tsp baking powder
1/2 tsp bicarbonate of soda
3/4 tsp mixed spice
a pinch of salt
1 medium orange, juice and
   finely grated zest
45 g (1 1/2 oz) butter, melted
1 egg
70 g (2 1/2 oz) soft light brown
   sugar
1 small courgette, finely grated
50 g (2 oz) raisins, chopped (can
   leave whole for older children)

I have chopped the raisins for the mini-muffins, making them easier for small children to eat, but you can leave them whole if baking regular-sized muffins.

Pre-heat the oven to 180°C/350°F/Gas 4/Fan 160°C. Line two mini-muffin tins with paper cases (or a 12-hole tin for regular muffins).

In a large bowl, stir together the flour, baking powder, bicarbonate of soda, mixed spice and a pinch of salt (omit for under 1 year olds). Set aside.

Measure the orange juice – you need 100 ml (3 1/2 fl oz). If it is less, then make up the quantity with milk or juice from a carton. Whisk the juice, zest, butter, egg and sugar together until well combined then stir into the flour mixture, followed by the courgette and raisins. Spoon into the muffin cases (fill almost to the top) and bake 12–14 minutes (increase the baking time to 22–25 minutes for regular-sized muffins), until firm to the touch. Cool on a wire rack. Store in an airtight container for up to 3 days.

Cinnamon Rolls

As they bake, these rolls fill the house with the delicious scent of cinnamon – perfect at breakfast or teatime. Their small size make them particularly child-friendly.

Beat the butter, sugar and cinnamon until well combined. Roll out the dough into a rectangle approximately 35 cm x 18 cm (14 in x 7 in) and transfer to a lightly floured board or work surface. Spread the cinnamon butter over the surface, leaving a 1 cm (½ in) border on one of the long edges. Roll up the dough into a long cylinder, starting from the long edge with the cinnamon butter and pressing gently to seal the dough roll.

Pre-heat the oven to 180°C/350°F/Gas 4/Fan 160°C. Cut the cylinder into 12 slices with a sharp knife that has been lightly dusted with flour. Arrange cut side up, on a lightly oiled baking sheet, in a rectangle of four rolls across and three rolls down, 1 cm (½ in) apart and the seams facing inwards. Cover with a clean, damp cloth and leave to rise for 15–20 minutes, until puffy and doubled in size (the rolls should touch each other slightly).

Brush the tops and sides of the rolls with a little of the beaten egg and bake for 18–20 minutes, until the rolls are golden and the bases sound hollow when tapped. Leave to cool slightly on the baking sheet.

Put the icing sugar in a small bowl and add the water, a few drops at a time, until you have a thick but pourable icing. Drizzle over the rolls then break them into individual portions. The rolls are nicest served warm. Leftover rolls can be stored for 1 day in an airtight container – gently reheat by putting in an oven pre-heated to 100°C/210°F/Gas ¼/Fan 80°C for 5 minutes.

🍲 Preparation 35 minutes, plus rising
🕐 Cook 20 minutes
🍥 Makes 12 small rolls
❄ Suitable for freezing: can be frozen either as dough or (un-iced) after baking. Reheat according to the method, left.

25 g (1 oz) butter, softened
25 g (1 oz) soft light brown sugar
½ tsp ground cinnamon
1 quantity Basic Bread Dough (see p. 115), replacing the olive oil with 15 g (½ oz) melted butter
1 egg, beaten

For the icing
4 tbsp icing sugar
approx. 1 tsp water

Super Strawberry Yoghurt Ripple Cornets

🖐 Preparation 15 minutes,
plus churning and freezing
🍽 Makes 6–8 portions
☺ Suitable for children
under 1 year old

225 g (8 oz) strawberries,
   hulled and halved
½ tsp fresh lemon juice
50 g (2 oz) caster sugar
400 g (14 oz) full fat natural
   yoghurt
150 g (5 oz) good quality
   strawberry jam (I used
   Bonne Maman)
200 ml (7 fl oz) double cream
ice-cream cornets, to serve

Ice-cream cornets are irresistible to all age groups – and making ice cream with yoghurt is extremely easy as you can just mix everything together. I love strawberry ice cream and strawberry sorbet – and this ripple ice cream gives me a little of each!

Put the strawberries, lemon juice and half of the sugar in a blender, and whiz to a purée. Taste the purée and add more of the sugar to sweeten, if necessary. You can sieve the purée to remove the seeds if you like. You should have around 200 ml (7 fl oz) of purée.

Put the yoghurt in a large bowl and stir in the jam plus half of the purée. Whip the cream to soft peaks in a separate bowl then fold the cream into the yoghurt mixture. Pour this ice-cream base into an ice-cream maker and churn according to the manufacturer's instructions.

Transfer the frozen ice cream to a re-sealable container. Spoon over the remaining strawberry purée and ripple though the ice cream with a knife or metal skewer. Cover and store in the freezer for up to 1 month.

To serve, scoop balls of the ice cream into cornets. If the ice cream is too hard to scoop then let it soften slightly at room temperature for 5–10 minutes.

Brownie Bites

Pre-heat the oven to 180°C/350°F/Gas 4/Fan 160°C. Line the base and sides of a 28 cm x 20 cm (14 in x 8 in) brownie tin with non-stick baking parchment.

Put the plain chocolate, butter and sugar in a heatproof bowl, and melt over a pan of warm water (don't let the bottom of the bowl touch the water). Alternatively, melt in the microwave in 15-second bursts, stirring between bursts. Set aside to cool.

Whisk together the eggs and vanilla, until just combined. Stir into the cooled chocolate then sift over the flour, cocoa, baking powder and salt, and mix in. Pour the batter into the prepared tin and bake for 25–30 minutes, until a skewer inserted into the centre comes out with damp crumbs clinging to it (but not uncooked brownie batter) – try not to over bake. Remove from the oven and leave to cool in the tin.

When the brownie base is cold, make the topping. Put the milk or plain chocolate, butter and cream in a heatproof bowl and carefully melt (as above). Stir until smooth then spread over the top of the brownie. Put the white chocolate in a separate bowl and carefully melt (as above). Spoon into the corner of a plastic food bag and snip off the corner then drizzle the white chocolate over the chocolate topping. Leave in a cool place (but not the fridge) until the topping is fully set.

Lift the brownie out of its tin, using the baking parchment. Put on a chopping board and cut into 16 bars (4 x 4) or 20 squares (4 x 5). Store in an airtight container in a cool place for up to 5 days.

Topping variation

You could melt 150 g (5 oz) milk chocolate and spread this over the top of the brownie, and when it's set pipe on words using the white-chocolate icing or white writing icing.

⏲ Preparation 30 minutes
🕐 Cook 30 minutes, plus cooling
🍮 Makes 16 small bars/20 small squares
❄ Suitable for freezing: lift the cold (un-iced) brownie from the tin and wrap (do not cut) in a double layer of cling film followed by a single layer of foil. Defrost for 2–3 hours at room temperature.

200 g (7 oz) plain chocolate, chopped
225 g (8 oz) butter, cut into cubes
250 g (9 oz) caster sugar
3 eggs
1 tsp vanilla extract
110 g (4 oz) flour
2 tbsp cocoa powder
1 tsp baking powder
1/4 tsp salt

For the topping
100 g (3 1/2 oz) milk or plain chocolate, chopped
15 g (1/2 oz) butter
2 tbsp double cream
50 g (2 oz) white chocolate, chopped

TIP
For a birthday, if you don't want to do a big cake, you could pile these up and pop a candle on top.

Apple and Mincemeat Streusel

🥣 Preparation 15 minutes
🕐 Cook 45 minutes
🍪 Makes 12 bars
❄ Suitable for freezing: wrap
the squares individually in cling
film and freeze in a re-sealable
box or freezer bag.

225 g (8 oz) flour
a pinch of salt
170 g (6 oz) butter
85 g (3 oz) ground almonds
85 g (3 oz) light soft brown sugar
½ tsp ground cinnamon
1 eating apple, peeled, quartered
    and cubed
410 g jar mincemeat

I like the combination of apple with mincemeat. You can buy mincemeat in jars in the supermarket, and there are now some quite exotic varieties from which to choose, especially when it's close to Christmas.

Pre-heat the oven to 180°C/350°F/Gas 4/Fan 160°C and line a 20 cm x 20 cm (8 in x 8 in) baking tin with non-stick baking parchment.

Mix the flour with the salt and rub in the butter until it resembles coarse breadcrumbs. You can do this using a food processor, but be careful not to over process as it will form clumps.

Transfer the mixture into a bowl (if using a food processor) and stir in the ground almonds, brown sugar and ground cinnamon. Pack two-thirds of the crumb mixture into the prepared tin (but don't press it down too firmly).

Stir the apple into the mincemeat and spread over the crumb base. Sprinkle the remaining crumb mixture over the mincemeat and apple, and bake in the pre-heated oven for 40–50 minutes or until golden brown.

Allow the streusel bars to cook in the tin (about 15 minutes) before transferring them in the baking parchment to a wire rack to cool fully, then cut into squares.

Oat and Raisin Cookies

These cookies are not only delicious but also have a dose of wholegrains, with the wholemeal flour and rolled oats, which help to keep up energy levels.

Pre-heat the oven to 180°C/350°F/Gas 4/Fan 160°C. Beat together the butter, sugar and vanilla. Add all the dry ingredients and mix together. Form into balls using one tablespoon of the mixture and arrange spaced apart on two baking sheets lined with non-stick baking parchment.

Bake for about 12 minutes until golden. Allow to firm up a little before lifting on to a wire rack to cool completely.

Preparation 20 minutes
Cook 12 minutes
Makes 10 cookies
Suitable for freezing

50 g (2 oz) butter
40 g (1½ oz) soft light
   brown sugar
½ tsp vanilla extract
30 g (1 oz) wholemeal flour
30 g (1 oz) rolled oats
¼ tsp ground cinnamon
   or mixed spice
¼ tsp salt
a pinch of bicarbonate of soda
30 g (1 oz) raisins

Cottage Cheese Dip for Fruit

Cottage cheese is a great source of protein, but some children dislike the texture. However, you can blend the cheese until it is smooth to make a tasty dip for chunks of fruit. Add a swirl of fruit purée for a splash of colour.

Blend the cottage cheese, milk and honey together until smooth. Cover and chill the dip until ready to serve (it will keep in the fridge for 3–4 days).

To serve, spoon two or three tablespoons of the dip into small containers, top with a teaspoon of fruit purée and swirl with a cocktail stick. Serve with chunks of your child's favourite fruits, for dipping.

Preparation 5 minutes
Makes 4–6 portions
Not suitable for freezing

200 g (7 oz) cottage cheese
   (not the fat-free type)
2 tbsp milk
1 tsp clear honey
4–6 tsp fruit compote or jam,
   to serve
fruit chunks (e.g. apple slices,
   halved strawberries,
   pineapple chunks), to serve

Hand-held Apple Pies

🍽 Preparation 30 minutes, plus cooling
🕐 Cook 15 minutes, plus cooling
🍥 Makes 6 pies
❄ Suitable for freezing: put the uncooked pies on a baking sheet lined with clingfilm. Cover with more clingfilm and freeze for 3–4 hours, until solid, then transfer to a freezer container. Bake direct from frozen in an oven pre-heated to 180°C/350°F/Gas 4/Fan 160°C on a well-greased baking sheet. Brush the tops with melted butter, bake for 20 minutes, then increase the oven to 200°C/400°F/Gas 6/Fan 180°C and bake for a further 5–8 minutes, until golden. Not suitable for reheating: best eaten freshly baked, so extras should be frozen, unbaked, and cooked from frozen.

2 large eating apples, peeled and cored (I use Pink Lady)
2 tbsp soft light brown sugar
¼ tsp ground cinnamon
50 g (2 oz) butter, melted
6 large sheets filo pastry
1 tsp icing sugar, to serve

TIP
I like to grate the apple as it is easier for small children to eat.

I have to admit it – these are inspired by the hand-held apple pies sold in a fast-food restaurant. But I have replaced the heavy pastry with light, crispy filo pastry and filled them with cinnamon-scented apple that isn't at all 'gloopy'. Filo can dry out quickly, so keep the sheets covered with a damp tea towel.

Grate the apples into a microwavable bowl, add the sugar and cinnamon, and toss to mix. Cover with cling film, punch a steam hole and microwave for 3–4 minutes, until the apples are softening but not mushy. Alternatively, simmer the apples in a small pan for 4–5 minutes. Uncover and leave to stand until cool, about 30 minutes.

Pre-heat the oven to 200°C/400°F/Gas 6/Fan 180°C. Grease a baking sheet with a little of the melted butter.

Lay one filo sheet on a flat work surface and brush the surface generously with melted butter. Fold in half (short end to short end) and brush the surface again with butter. Put a rounded tablespoonful of the apple filling at one of the short ends of the folded filo and spread out slightly, leaving a 2 cm (¾ in) border on either side. Fold in the two long sides (partially covering the filling at the bottom) and brush the folded-in margins with butter. Roll up from the filled end to make a cylinder. Sit the pie, seam side down, on the prepared baking sheet and cover with a lightly dampened tea towel or kitchen paper. Repeat with the remaining filo, butter and apple.

Brush the tops and sides with butter and bake for 10–15 minutes, until golden. Allow to cool for around 30 minutes then dust with icing sugar. The filling can remain very hot so I prefer to cut the pies in half to serve.

Mini Jam Tarts

Jewel-bright jam tarts are a yummy and easy-to-eat teatime treat but can also be packed into lunchboxes. You can buy some very good sugar-free jams.

Pre-heat the oven to 180°C/350°F/Gas 4/Fan 160°C.

Lay the pastry on a flat surface and use a 5 cm (2 in) round cutter to cut out 24 pastry circles. Gently push the pastry circles into the cups of mini-muffin tins.

Drop half a teaspoonful of jam into the centre of each pastry shell then bake the tarts for 18–20 minutes, until the pastry is golden. Cool for 5 minutes in the tin then transfer to a wire rack to cool further. If eating warm, check the temperature of the tarts before serving, as the jam can get very hot. Store cooled tarts in an airtight container for 2–3 days.

Preparation 15 minutes
Cook 20 minutes
Makes 24 tarts
Suitable for freezing: put cooled tarts in a single layer in a re-sealable box and freeze. Defrost for 1–2 hours. Reheat for 10 minutes in an oven pre-heated to 110°C/225°F/ Gas ¼/ Fan 90°C.

1 x 375 g block ready rolled shortcrust pastry
approx. 150 g (5 oz) jam

Carrot Cupcakes

🍵 Preparation 15 minutes
🕐 Cook 22 minutes
🍩 Makes 16 cupcakes
😊 Suitable for children under 1 year old
❄ Suitable for freezing (baked but un-iced) cupcakes can be frozen for up to 1 month. Defrost for 2–3 hours at room temperature.

170 g (6 oz) self-raising flour
1/2 tsp bicarbonate of soda
1 tsp mixed spice
a pinch of salt
170 g (6 oz) butter, at room temperature
170 g (6 oz) soft light brown sugar
3 eggs, beaten
1/2 tsp vanilla extract
2 tbsp soured cream or Greek yoghurt
140 g (5 oz) grated carrot
110 g (4 oz) raisins

For the icing
140 g (5 oz) icing sugar
4 tbsp maple syrup
3/4 tsp water
30 g (1 oz) pecan nuts, chopped (optional), to decorate

Making cupcakes gives toddlers a more manageable 'personal' cake than the traditional large, sliced carrot cake. You could also bake these in ring moulds on a baking sheet so that they look like mini carrot cakes with a swirl of icing on top.

Pre-heat the oven to 190°C/375°F/Gas 5/Fan 170°C. Line two regular-size muffin tins with 16 paper cases.

Sift together the flour, bicarbonate of soda, mixed spice and salt, and set aside. Put the butter and sugar in a large bowl and beat until fluffy. Add the eggs, vanilla, soured cream and sifted dry ingredients, and beat until just combined. Fold in the carrot and raisins.

Spoon the cake mix into the prepared muffin tins, filling each paper case around three-quarters full (an ice-cream scoop is good for this). Bake for 18–22 minutes, until a cocktail stick inserted into the centre of the cupcakes comes out clean. Cool for 5 minutes in the tins, then transfer to a wire rack to cool completely.

To make the icing, put the icing sugar in a bowl and stir in the maple syrup. Add the water, a few drops at a time, to make an icing that will thickly coat the back of a spoon. Spread on to the cupcakes and sprinkle over the pecans (if using).

The iced cupcakes will keep in an airtight container for 3–4 days.

Ice Lollies

Fruity ice lollies are a great finger food, and one I often recommend to parents who have kids who refuse to eat fruit – they can be fooled by a frozen 'treat'! The high level of fruit makes these slightly soft, like a sorbet on a stick, so for teething babies it is best to add an extra 100 ml (3 fl oz) water to the orange juice, which will make the lollies icier and better for sore gums (it will make 600 ml/20 fl oz with the extra water).

Preparation 10 minutes, plus cooling and freezing
Cook 15 minutes
Makes about 500 ml (17 fl oz)

1 medium eating apple, peeled, cored and chopped
1 medium ripe pear, peeled, cored and chopped
110 g (4 oz) ready-to-eat dried apricots, chopped
120 ml (4 fl oz) water
30 g (1 oz) sugar
100 ml (3½ fl oz) fresh orange juice

Apple, Pear and Apricot Ice Lollies

Put the apple, pear, apricots and water in a medium pan. Add half of the sugar and put over a medium heat. Bring to a simmer then cover and cook for around 15 minutes, until the fruit is soft. Stir occasionally and add a little extra water if the fruit is looking too dry.

Transfer the cooked fruit to a blender and allow to cool slightly. Add the orange juice and blend until smooth – take care when blending hot liquids. Taste the fruit purée – it should be fairly sweet (and will taste much less sweet when frozen) – and add the remaining sugar if necessary.

Cool to room temperature then pour into lolly moulds and freeze overnight. Best used within 1 month. The purée is also delicious swirled into natural yoghurt.

Forest Fruits and Apple Ice Lollies

Berries and apple go well together in a crumble but are also perfect partners in an ice lolly.

Preparation 5 minutes, plus cooling and freezing
Cook 5–7 minutes
Makes 400 ml (14 fl oz)
Suitable for children under 1 year old

Peel, core and dice the apples and put them in a medium pan with the berries and water. Heat gently until the berries have released some juice, then bring up to a boil and simmer for 5–7 minutes, until the apple is soft.

Remove from the heat and stir in the sugar until dissolved. Taste the fruit and add a little more sugar if it is too sharp (this will depend on how ripe the berries are). Purée the fruit and sieve to remove the seeds. Cool then pour into lolly moulds and freeze overnight.

2 medium eating apples
   (we used Fuji)
450 g (1 lb) mixed forest fruits
   (e.g. strawberries,
   blackberries, raspberries,
   blackcurrants), fresh or frozen
2 tbsp water
75 g (2½ oz) sugar

Mango, Pineapple and Orange Ice Lollies

A fun way to use up a slightly over-ripe mango, these lollies can give a little burst of tropical sunshine in winter months.

Preparation 5 minutes, plus freezing
Makes about 250 ml (8 fl oz)
Suitable for children under 1 year old

Put all of the ingredients in a blender and whiz until smooth. If your mango isn't very ripe then you may need to add an extra tablespoonful of sugar. Pour into lolly moulds and freeze overnight.

1 small very ripe mango, peeled,
   stoned and diced
1 x 225 g can crushed pineapple,
   well drained (use cubed
   pineapple if you can't find
   crushed)
3 tbsp fresh orange juice
   (from a carton is also fine)
50 g (2 oz) sugar

'Traffic Light' Fruit Skewers with Creamy Caramel Dip

🍲 Preparation 10 minutes
🍥 Makes 8 skewers or
4 portions
❄ Not suitable for freezing

¼ galia or other green
    melon, seeded
½ large mango, peeled,
    or approx. 140 g (5 oz)
    ready-prepared mango
8 medium strawberries, hulled

For the creamy caramel dip
4 tbsp dulce de leche
4 tsp double cream
You will also need 8 plastic
    or wooden skewers

The red, yellow and green of these fruits make for an attractive presentation that will appeal to children, but you can use any combination of fruits that your child particularly enjoys.

Remove the rind from the melon and cut into eight cubes, each approximately 2.5 cm (1 in). Cut the mango into eight similar-sized cubes. Thread one cube of melon on to each skewer, followed by a cube of mango and a strawberry.
  Mix together the dulce de leche and cream to make the dip, and spoon into small bowls. Serve with the fruit skewers.

Lemon Yoghurt Dip Variation
For a tasty, alternative dip that is easy to prepare, mix 6 tablespoons thick Greek yoghurt with 2 teaspoons milk, 2 teaspoons icing sugar and 2 tablespoons lemon curd.

Index

Annabel Karmel is the leading expert on creating healthy food that children like to eat and tasty family meals that don't require parents to spend hours in the kitchen. After the tragic loss of her first child, Natasha, who died of a rare viral disease aged just three months, Annabel wrote her first book, *The Complete Baby and Toddler Meal Planner*, which has become the definitive guide on feeding babies and toddlers and is now sold all over the world. Annabel appears frequently on radio and television as the UK's expert on children's nutritional issues and writes regularly for national newspapers and magazines. Her website, annabelkarmel. com, is the no.1 site for information and recipes on healthy food for children and has become one of the fastest-growing resources for mothers, with thousands of members chatting live every day. Annabel was awarded an MBE in 2006 for her outstanding services to child nutrition.

For more information visit www.annabelkarmel.com

Acknowledgements

My children Nicholas, Lara and Scarlett, who now don't remember how to use a knife and fork. Caroline Brewster, Marina Magpoc and Letty Catada, for fun times in the kitchen assisting me in testing the recipes for the book. Seiko Hatfield, my wonderful food stylist. Dave King for his magical photography and styling. Jo Harris for the props. Tripp Trapp for the high chairs. My mother, Evelyn Etkind, for her endless support. Everyone at Ebury, including Carey Smith, Fiona MacIntyre, Judith Hannam, Sarah Bennie and Helen Armitage. Mary Jones, my PR, for always being the bearer of good news. Everyone at Smith and Gilmour for designing such a beautiful book. And all the gorgeous models Alfie and Max Beer, Bibi Boundy, Sam Cooke, George Gates, Lily Smith and Somer Tong.

Growing up with Annabel Karmel
Books for every stage of your child's development.

As a parent, giving your child a healthy start in life is a top priority. Annabel offers a cookbook for every stage of your child's development. As the UK's number one bestselling author on cooking for babies and children, Annabel's tried and tested recipes and meal planners have proved invaluable to families for over 20 years.

Pregnancy

Family

Baby and Toddler

School age/cooking for kids

For more information go to **www.annabelkarmel.com**

Don't Get in a Mess!

by Sam Watkins and
Louise Forshaw

W
FRANKLIN WATTS
LONDON•SYDNEY

Franklin Watts

First published in Great Britain in 2016 by
The Watts Publishing Group

Text © Sam Watkins 2016
Illustrations © Louise Forshaw 2016

The rights of Sam Watkins to be identified as the
author and Louise Forshaw as the illustrator of this Work
have been asserted in accordance with the Copyright, Designs
and Patents Act, 1988.

Series Editor: Jackie Hamley
Series Advisor: Catherine Glavina
Series Designer: Peter Scoulding

A CIP catalogue record for this book is available
from the British Library.

ISBN 978 1 4451 4594 5 (hbk)
ISBN 978 1 4451 4587 7 (pbk)
ISBN 978 1 4451 4593 8 (library ebook)

Printed in China

FSC
www.fsc.org
MIX
Paper from
responsible sources
FSC® C104740

Franklin Watts
An imprint of
Hachette Children's Group
Part of The Watts Publishing Group
Carmelite House
50 Victoria Embankment
London EC4Y 0DZ

An Hachette UK company.
www.hachette.co.uk

www.franklinwatts.co.uk

"I'm bored," said Tom.

Dad looked up from his newspaper. "Why don't you play outside?" he said.

"It's raining," said Liza.
"Splish, splosh," said Ollie,
their little brother.

"I know, let's do some painting," said Liza.

Tom got the painting stuff.

"Don't get in a mess," said Dad and went back to his paper.

Liza painted a dinosaur.

Tom painted a castle.

Ollie painted his hands
green.

"Ollie!" whispered Liza. "Dad said, 'don't get in a mess!'"

Tom painted an elephant.

Liza painted a giraffe.

Ollie painted his face green. "Raaah," said Ollie. "I'm a monster!"

Liza giggled. Ollie looked
so funny!

Liza painted her face white. "Wooooo! I'm a ghost," she said.

18

19

Tom painted his face
yellow with black stripes.

"Grrrrr! I'm a tiger,"
he said.

Dad looked over his paper. "I thought I said *not* to get in a mess!"

23

The ghost and the tiger
looked at each other.

"Raaah," said the monster.

Dad shook his head.
"I think it's time to play
outside now!" he said.

"But Dad, it's still raining," said Tom.

"Exactly!" said Dad.

28

Puzzle 1

a

b

c

d

e

f

Put these pictures in the correct order.
Now tell the story in your own words.
Can you think of a different ending?

Puzzle 2

bored   fed up

scared

shocked   jolly

surprised

Choose the words which best describe Tom and which best describe his dad in the pictures. Can you think of any more?

Answers

Puzzle 1

The correct order is:

1b, 2d, 3e, 4a, 5c, 6f

Puzzle 2

Tom   The correct words are bored, fed up.

The incorrect word is scared.

Dad   The correct words are shocked, surprised.

The incorrect word is jolly.

Look out for more stories:

Bill's Silly Hat
ISBN 978 1 4451 1617 4

Little Joe's Boat Race
ISBN 978 0 7496 9467 8

Little Joe's Horse Race
ISBN 978 1 4451 1619 8

Felix, Puss in Boots
ISBN 978 1 4451 1621 1

Cheeky Monkey's Big Race
ISBN 978 1 4451 1618 1

The Animals' Football Cup
ISBN 978 0 7496 9477 7

The Animals' Football Camp
ISBN 978 1 4451 1616 7

The Animals' Football Final
ISBN 978 1 4451 3879 4

That Noise!
ISBN 978 0 7496 9479 1

The Frog Prince and the Kitten
ISBN 978 1 4451 1620 4

Gerald's Busy Day
ISBN 978 1 4451 3939 5

Dani's Dinosaur
ISBN 978 1 4451 3945 6

The Cowboy Kid
ISBN 978 1 4451 3949 4

Robbie's Robot
ISBN 978 1 4451 3953 1

The Green Machines
ISBN 978 1 4451 3957 9

For details of all our titles go to: www.franklinwatts.co.uk